MUSLIM MINORITY CONTINUITY AND CHANGE

MUSLIM MINORITY
Continuity and Change

Asghar Ali Engineer

GYAN PUBLISHING HOUSE
NEW DELHI-110002

Muslim Minority : Continuity and Change

Rs. 540

ISBN: 978-81-212-1013-3

Published in 2009 in India by
Gyan Publishing House
24, Main Ansari Road, Darya Ganj,
New Delhi-110002
Phones : 23282060, 23261060
Fax : 011-23285914
E-mail: books@gyanbooks.com
Website: www.gyanbooks.com

Lasser Type Setting by: Rudra Computer Graphics, Delhi
Printed at : G. Print Process, Delhi

Contents

Preface

Here in this book I have collected my articles written from time to time in fortnightly Secular Perspective. These articles deal with communal and secular problems, peace, communal harmony and problems faced by minorities. Ours is a constitutional democracy and Constitution has guaranteed certain fundamental rights to all the citizens of India and certain religious and cultural rights to religious and linguistic minorities.

These fundamental and religious and linguistic rights are most important for smooth functioning of democracy. But to guarantee rights in the Constitution is one thing and to implement them in a country with bewildering diversity and clashing communal and linguistic interests is something else. In all the countries religious and linguistic minorities establish their hegemony and deny these basic rights to minorities. One has to constantly struggle for realization of these rights in the interest of unity and national integrity.

In India we also have problem of communalism and communal violence. Often communal violence breaks out on petty matters between Hindus and Muslims and our law and order machinery is also far from being ideal. Again conscious citizens have to struggle to maintain peace in the country and ensure justice to those who are victims of the violence.

These essays have been written from time to time on these problems in response to different situations arising in the country. These articles put together can map the minority situation in the country and can also provide roadmap for implementation of our constitutional values in practice. Yes, opinions can differ on controversial issues and it is not necessary that everyone will agree with the opinions expressed in these articles. But in a democracy different points of view must b e debated freely and honestly. It will help enrich our political discourse.

Also, every community has internal problems, political, religious, social and cultural. Indian Muslims are also faced with many internal problems, especially of religious and social nature. Many social reforms are needed to be carried out. To live in a secular society, one has to respond to new socio-cultural challenges in a creative way. Change is the law of life. Muslims cannot remain stagnant.

Many articles in this collection relate to problems of socio-religious nature and on the urgency of religious and social reforms particularly pertaining to women. Some of these articles discuss these problems and advocate change in shari'ah laws of divorce, polygamy etc. Muslim women, in a secular and democratic society, must enjoy those rights which other women do. And these rights are available to women even within Islamic frame-work, if certain basic reforms are carried out. Some of these articles discuss the need to carry out these reforms.

Thus this book would enable readers to understand minority situation in Indian politically, socially and from religious perspective as well. I hope the book will be useful both for lay readers as well as for academics and students of secularism in India.

Asghar Ali Engineer

1

First War of Indepedence in 1857- Its Impact on Hindu-Muslim Relations

India is celebrating this year 150 years of our first war of independence though the Britishers naturally called it 'mutiny'. But we Indians prefer to call it our first war of independence. Of course there is serious problem too, when we refer it to war of independence. Was India a nation at that point of time? Also, can we call it a struggle for independence when in fact some rajas and nawabs or feudal lords were fighting for their respective territory or landed estate? Even Marx wrote it was a revolt by feudal lords.

Tara Chand, a noted scholar writes in his *History of Freedom Movement in India* (vol. II, pp. 42) "It has to be admitted that the war against the British was not inspired by any sentiment of nationalism, for in 1857 India was not yet politically a nation. It is a fact that the Hindus and Muslims co-operated, but the leaders and the followers of the two communities were moved by personal loyalties rather than loyalty to a common motherland."

Of course this is one side. The other side is that it was a unique struggle in which both feudal lords as well as common people fought together. There was as much anger amongst feudal lords as among common people, may be for different reasons. But no one can deny surging sentiments against the British as foreign rulers. Tara Chand also admits this when he writes: "The uprising of 1857 was a general movement of the traditional *elite* of the Muslims and the Hindus – princess, landlords, soldiers, scholars and theologians (Pandits and Maulavis). The Emperor of Delhi, the King of Oudh, some Nawabs and Rajas, Talukadars and Zamindars, the soldiers – Pathans (Walaytis), Mughals, Rajputs and Brahmans of northern India – and the maulavis who were members of this order, comprised the main body of rebels." (Tarachand, op. ct. p. 43)

Though each category of rebels had its own reasons to participate in the rebellion, they together were quite a representative group. In those days leadership could be taken only by feudal –lords, as they constituted the ruling class. But what is important to note is that they had common people lined up behind them. It is true India was not a nation then but India as a country did exist and all coming together, at least from north India made it quite a representative group. It is also true, as Percival Spear points out "The passions of the mutineers were centred on their grievances, not on larger ideals." Perhaps that was the reason why they did not succeed.

Another thing to be noted is that it represented the spectacle of Hindu-Muslim unity and Hindus themselves chose the Moghul Emperor as the leader of the movement. This fact had its own symbolic value. The significance of Hindu-Muslim unity was not lost on the Britishers and after failure of the revolt, they systematically devised ways and means to divide Hindus and Muslims. We are paying price for that until today though the reasons for division between Hinds and Muslims are more of our own making.

We are here concerned more with the aftermath of 1857 struggle than the struggle itself. In fact consolidation of British rule after failure of our war of independence was a mixed bag. It undoubtedly strengthened our slavery to a foreign power but also brought some benefits. We were exposed to modern education and rational and scientific ideas. Modern ideas came to be imbibed by a section of Indians though there was stiff opposition to them by traditionalists. Sati came to be outlawed thanks to the efforts of Raja Ram Mohan Roy. Many Muslim reformers also came to the fore.

Many thinkers and intellectuals found themselves in the midst of tension between tradition and modernity. It was very aptly expressed by the great poet Ghalib when he says, in one of his *ghazals*: *Iman mujhe roke hai to khinche he mujhe kufr – Ka'ba mere piche hai to kalisa mere aage* [iman (belief in Islam) stops me and kufr (British progress and rationalism) pulls me]. Thus the holiest mosque Ka'ba is behind me and church is ahead of me.) This was very apt description of situation confronting many thinkers and intellectuals of time.

Some insist that while Hindus produced social and religious reformers who stressed modern education, Muslims continued to cling to older ways and refused to accept change. This is at best, very superficial approach, even prejudiced, in many cases. Muslims also produced great reformers though their impact was not as widespread as those of Hindu reformers, for various reasons. We will throw light on some of these reasons.

Generally name of Sir Syed Ahmed Khan is well known as social reformer and educationist but he was not alone. Many more wrote extensively to advocate modern reforms like Maulavi Mumtaz Ali Khan, Maulavi Chiragh Ali, Sheikh Abdullah, Justice Ameer Ali and several others.

It is not very well- known that Maulavi Mumtaz Ali Khan was a great advocate of Muslim women's rights. He wrote a remarkable book *Huququn Niswan* (Rights of Women). Maulavi Mumtaz Ali was contemporary of Sir Syed. He believed in complete equality of men and women and argued his case for gender equality on the basis of Qur'an and hadith, something unthinkable in those days when women were completely subordinated. Maulavi Saheb also began to publish a journal of women of which his wife was editor and after her death his daughter took charge of the magazine.

The book *Huququn Niswan* was so revolutionary in its approach that even Sir Syed advised Mumtaz Ali Khan not to publish it lest it should cause more problems for him. In fact Sir Syed himself was an advocate of women's rights as is evident from his incomplete commentary on Holy Qur'an but he had to give up his project of completing the commentary under pressure from orthodox 'Ulama in return winning their support for his MAO College which he was trying to establish in Aligarh.

However, Maulavi Mumtaz Ali Khan had passionate conviction for gender equality and he did publish the book despite opposition from Sir Syed. Similarly Sheikh Abdullah advocated women's education and established a women's school in Aligarh which flowered later into full-fledged women's college which today is part of Aligarh Muslim University. Maulavi Chiragh Ali also wrote for reforms in Muslim personal law so did Justice Ameer Ali. Ameer Ai's book *Spirit of Islam* is a significant contribution in this respect. Though there was some resistance to modern education in North Indian Muslims thanks to influence of orthodox 'ulama, there was absolutely no such resistance in South India. In Bombay Justice Badruddin Tyebji established Anjuman-e-Islam school; for modern education, an organisation which has several educational institutions today. This contrast is interesting as in north India the 'ulama had lost all influence and offices of religious education in Moghul court or regional Muslim rulers, in Bombay and elsewhere in South Muslims generally benefited from modern education in commercial cities like Bombay.

The reason why there was stiff opposition to modern education and social reforms and its limited impact was that there was no emergent class among Muslims like capitalist class or entrepreneur class among Muslims to immediately benefit from modern reforms. The ruling class among Muslims was mainly feudal and this class was more or less ruined after 1857. This class also borne the brunt of British wrath as it was seen as leading the revolt. Of course later the British rulers tried to co-opt this class to stem the rising tide of Hindu nationalism.

On the other hand there was the Muslim artisan class in urban and semi urban areas of north India. To this class, modern education made hardly any sense. There was no idle class aspiring for modern education and modern reforms. There was total absence of modern entrepreneur class among Muslims in north India, which, among Hindus, was emerging.

The British rule, as pointed out above, resulted in serious cleavage between Hindus and Muslims because of British policy on one hand, and for indigenous reasons, on the other. Such cleavage never existed before. There was composite ruling class, which shared power at various levels of feudal hierarchy. Now there began to emerge new consciousness of separate interests and separate identities.

Competitive examinations for British administrative jobs, language controversies (Urdu-Hindi), tablighi and shuddhi movements, all this went a long way to divide us. When the Indian National Congress was formed which once again tried to unite Hindus and Muslims, the British used some *Zamindars* and *Jagirdars* to form Indian Muslim League in 1906. This became particularly necessary as the 'Ulama, under the leadership of Maulaa Qasim Ahmed Nanotvi supported Indian National Congress by issuing a *fatwa* urging Muslims to join INC. The Maulana, not only issued fatwa himself but collected 100 such *fatwas* and compiled them under the title of *Nsrat al-*

Ahrar (for help of freedom fighters). This alarmed the British rulers and they thought it necessary to float Indian Union Muslim League through the agency of some Muslim Zamindars and Jagirdars.

Sir Syed, it must be said, was all along great champion of Hindu-Muslim unity and had even solicited donations from his Hindu friends for MAO college project. But due to language controversy his relations were strained with his Hindu friends. But it is too much to describe him as founder of two- nation theory. It is not borne out of any of his writings. The use of words like Hindu qaum or Muslim qaum never implied two separate nations. It was used in those days in the sense of community and not nation.

2

Divorce in Qur'an and Shari'ah

The other day I read an article on divorce in *Inquilab,* an Urdu Daily from Mumbai written by a well known 'alim and member of Muslim Personal Law Board Khalid Saifullah Rahmani. The title of the article was "Ghusse ki haalat ka f'al m'utabar hota hai to talaq kyun m'utabar nahin hogi" i.e. if generally anything done in anger is valid why not a divorce given in anger? If any lay person had written this article even then it would have been considered outrageous and when written by one who is considered an 'alim, it is much more so.

The Maulana argues that generally divorce is given in state of anger only and he argues if a husband is happy with his wife, will he gift her divorce? Divorce is given only when husband gets angry with his wife due to some act of hers. And then he says not only divorce but also several things are done in the state of anger. One would not like to comment on such arguments had it not involved fate of hundreds of Muslim women. One can only ring ones hands at such status of our prominent 'ulama. They take divorce so lightly and break up of family for them is only a matter of husband's anger with his wife.

Maulana Rahmani also maintains in this article that all *fuqaha'* have consensus that divorce takes place if given in state of anger because in this state as in this state man remains conscious of his act. Then the Maulana goes on to quote noted jurist Allama Abidayn Shami who has quoted Hafiz ibn Qayyim (very well known jurist and 'alim and disciple of Ibn Taymiyyah) and argues that anger has three stages: one that no change has occurred in his reasoning power due to anger and what he says, he should be understanding that and he should remain aware of its consequences and divorce pronounced in this state of anger will be valid. Second state is of extreme anger when man is unable to understand consequences of what he is doing and lacks in his will power. In this status divorce will not be valid since such a status of anger borders on madness and divorce given in a state of madness is not valid. Third state of anger is between the two states i.e. when man is partially aware of what he is saying and doing and partially not and divorce given in this state will also not be valid.

These are hardly acceptable arguments and at best these are rationalization or justification of divorce given in a state of anger. One would like to ask Maulana and the jurists he quotes who will determine what state of anger one is when pronouncing divorce? Is there any objective criteria available to measure husband's anger at the time of pronouncing divorce? Has any instrument like thermometer available for measuring the degree of anger? And for these jurists even two witnesses for divorce are not necessary as prescribed by the Qur'an?

A divorce simply takes place if a husband pronounces divorce thrice in one breathe and no witnesses are required. If witnesses are not required who will bear witness as to which state of anger divorce was pronounced? Will husband's own statement will be relied on? And if husband is determined to divorce his wife, how can his statement as to what state of anger he was in at the time of divorce can be acceptable. Who will decide what state of anger he was at the time of pronouncing divorce? Very strange rationalization indeed for justifying divorce in a state of anger.

Also, these arguments are completely at variance with what Qur'an says about divorce. Firstly, Qur'an requires, as pointed out earlier, two witnesses for divorce. Also, there is not even indirect evidence in Qur'an for giving divorce in a state of anger. See these two verses of Qur'an from Chapter 65 (Surah Al-Talaq) "O Prophet, when you divorce women, divorce them for their prescribed period, and calculate the period; and keep your duty to Allah, your Lord. Turn them not out of their houses – nor should they themselves go away – unless they commit an open indecency. And these are limits of Allah. And whoever goes beyond limits of Allah, he indeed wrongs his own soul..." (65:1)

And we find in second verse of this chapter (65), "So when they have reached their prescribed time, retain them with kindness or **dismiss them with kindness,** and **call to witness two just ones from among you, and give upright; testimony for Allah**. With that is admonished he who believes in Allah and the latter Day. And whoever keeps his duty to Allah, He ordains a way out for him.

Let Maulana Rahmani note that Qur'an not only does not talk of divorcing in a state of anger but requires husband to divorce her (*fariquhunna*) with **kindness**. Also, she should not be thrown out of her marital home by the husband nor should she herself leave her marital home unless she comes with an indecent act (*bi fahishatin*). Also, Qur'an wherever talks of divorce, requires husbands to divorce them or separate them, with kindness. The verse 229 of Chapter 2 also talks of kindness while letting them go or separating them.

The verse is as under:" Divorce may be (pronounced) twice; then keep them in good fellowship (*bi m'arufin*) or let (them) go with kindness (*tasrihun bi ihsan*). Also so ensure full justice for women Qur'an requires arbitration before divorce (4:35). Thus there cannot be fairer method for divorce than the one prescribed by the Qur'an.

It is so unfortunate that Muslim jurists, under the influence of patriarchal ethos of their societies, they ignored all Qur'an injunctions and gave more credence to prevalent social practices and that too in the name of Islam. All this corpus of laws are referred to as Islamic laws of divine origin. In total contradiction to what Qur'an prescribes, the jurists, not only justified divorce given in a state of anger but also described states of anger.

What is more central to Islam - justice (*'adl, qist*) or state of proper consciousness in anger? Forget about anger, Qur'an does not approve of divorce in normal state of consciousness if proper method is not followed for giving divorce which ensures justice for wife. Any unjust act is *zulm* (oppression, wrong doing). According to the Qur'an women must be treated with fairness and justice and no act, committed in a state of anger (whatever the state of anger) can be a just act.

Maulana Rahmani's argument is very strange indeed that husband if not in a state of anger, will he divorce when he is happy with wife? Divorce, in fact should never be given in a state of anger at all. Whatever state of anger, intense, extreme or moderate, one does loose control of oneself and even if he is conscious of consequences of his act, is unable to think coolly and rationally. And Qur'an requires husband to remain kind even when divorcing her. Can anyone be kind while pronouncing divorce in a state of anger? Kindness and anger are two opposite states of mind.

Also, there are several instances in which husband pronounce divorce on getting angry on petty quarrels with wife.

Can then such divorces be justified? Often husband repents after pronouncing divorce thrice in a state of anger but our jurists maintain his wife has been irrevocably divorced and he cannot take her back unless she marries some other man and he divorces her.

Husband and wife often quarrel and husband gets angry temporarily and is provoked to pronounce divorce. So such petty quarrels would become basis for divorce. This is not only legally wrong but also morally totally wrong. But such are our jurists and 'responsible' members of personal law board. Can Muslim women then ever expect justice from them?

On one hand these jurists will argue that Islam greatly raised status of women and in pre-Islamic society women were treated as chattels and, on the other hand, to maintain manly authority, bring back those pre-Islamic practices in divine garb. Qur'an put the entire responsibility of treating women fairly and with kindness on men and our jurists gave total authority to men to throw their wives away whenever they liked.

There is not a single verse in Qur'an which exhorts women to treat their husbands with kindness while in their nikah (marital bond) whereas there are several verses requiring men to treat their wives with kindness. This was because women were in weaker position in that society and Islam has all the sympathy for weaker sections of society. In fact Islam lad greatest stress on giving justice to weaker sections of society including slaves, servants, orphan, widows and the poor.

As we have repeatedly pointed out Qur'an's sympathy is with *mustad'ifin* (those who have been weakened) (5:28) and our Ulama show all the sympathy with men who had all the power over women in that society (and still this continues even in most modern society) and juristically gives all the power over them. Let us remember justice is more central than opinion of any jurist howsoever eminent that jurist may be. Justice is Qur'an's central principle which cannot be sacrificed on the altar of any jurist's opinion.

If we have to project Islam as religion of justice and compassion for weaker sections of society we will have to revise our jurisprudence completely and prioritize justice over opinions of all past jurists of eminence. Eminence is not a principle it is only a social status whereas justice is a moral value central to Islam. Divorce is a very serious act and should be treated with utmost caution and responsibility. It breaks families and causes trauma to wife and children. According to a well-known hadith Allah has permitted act of divorce with utmost reluctance. Thus neither Qur'an nor authentic hadith are problem for women, it is male authority which is.

3

BJP's Anti -Muslimism

The CD controversy in U.P. election has proved once again, if any proof is needed, how much BJP hates Muslims. BJP's anti-Muslim record has touched new heights. How can any politically responsible party taking part in democratic election and taking oath for secularism, can produce such propaganda stuff. The CD is full of hate for Muslims and uses very derogatory language. The only parallel one can find is Nazi's hate of Jews, no other example could be found.

It celebrates any anti-Muslim measure or judgement. Recently when the single judge of Allahabad High Court declared Muslims in U.P. as not being a minority, the BJP spokesperson immediately welcomed the judgement as refutation of Congress party's 'minorityism' and vindication of BJP's stand. No other party welcomed the judgement and all other party's except the BJP criticised the judgement as unfair. The Judge had simply pronounced the judgement, which was not even relevant to the petition before him and he had not even given reasons for the judgement he delivered. The judgement was even against what the Supreme Court had held in TMA Pai Foundation judgement.

Right from post-independence days Muslims have been taken as constituting minority, though most major one. No one had ever expressed any doubt about it. The Supreme Court had held that any religious community less than 50% in number shall be deemed to be a minority and any all India -minority will also be deemed to be minority in any state. Also, as claimed by the honourable judge of Allahabad High Court, there are no such references in the Constitutional Assembly debates to prove that Muslims are not a minority in U.P. or any other state of Union of India.

Before all these matters were gone into BJP immediately welcomed the judgement and treated it as vindication of its stand on minorityism. One can as well tell BJP that the Congress whether indulges in minorityism or not BJP certainly indulges in anti-Muslimism. It whole-heartedly welcomes any anti-Muslim measure most enthusiastically.

In fact during the entire campaign for Ramjanmabhoomi BJP and many of its individual members like Sadhvi Rithambara and others indulged in most vicious anti-Muslim campaign. Cheap rhetoric of all Muslims being 'Babar ki Aulad' (Babar's children) was indulged in without any restraint. Uma Bharti and Rithambara used most abusive language against Muslims throughout Ramjanmaboomi campaign until Babri Masjid was demolished by a frenzied mob and when Masjid was demolished BJP leaders hugged each other in joy and celebrated the day as day of Diwali. Crackers were burst, especially in U.P. throughout that night.

Until today the Sangh Parivar celebrates it as '*Shaurya Divas*' (day of bravery) whereas whole country observes it as a tragic day in the history of secular India. And all this after the leaders of Jan Sangh, which was re-christened as Bhartiya Janta Party (BJP) had taken a vow on Gandhiji's Samadhi of following principles of Gandhian socialism and secularism. Soon after taking this oath in 1980 it started its anti-Muslim campaign describing constitutional secularism as pseudo-secularism and accused the Congress for indulging in 'minorityism' and fought subsequent elections with those slogans.

I sincerely advise BJP leaders to rename the party as BHP (Bhartiya Hindu Party) as it always excludes Muslims from people of India. Had it been sincerely Bhartiya Janata Party, it would have never adopted such anti-Muslim attitude towards Indian Muslims. Thus Hindu Mahasabha is more sincere in its ideology as it clearly designates itself as Hindu Party caring only for Hindu interests. And to this extent Hindu Mahasabha leaders disagree with BJP because the important word 'Hindu' is missing though it claims to be looking after Hindu interests.

The BJP leaders are trying to disown the CD under question only after the Election Commission took a strong view of the contents of the CD and said it is likely to promote disharmony between religious communities and issued notice to the BJP why action should not be taken against it. We congratulate the courage and principled stand taken by the Election Commission on this issue. It was overdue. Many prominent citizens have petitioned the Election Commission to de-recognise BJP as a political party as it always indulges in campaigns which endangers national unity and integrity.

Anyway any party, which publicly proclaims 'Hindutva Agenda' cannot be a secular party which it avows to be. Hindutva or Islamism in political arena for that matter cannot be in conformity with secularism. Secularism is basically a political doctrine. All political parties have to conform to secularism as a political philosophy and Election Commission requires all candidates filing nomination to take oath for secularism and political parties also have to declare their acceptance of it. How can then a party proclaiming 'Hindutva' doctrine be accepted as secular? It defies common sense.

The BJP often quotes one Judge Supreme Court Judgement that 'Hindutva' is a way of life. It may be so but it cannot be political way of life as our political way is nothing but secular, devoid of, or neutral to, any religious way of life or doctrines or interests only of one religion or followers thereof.

How can building a Ram Temple be agenda of a secular political party though uniform civil code and abolition of Article 370 are quite secular in nature? Building Ram temple, howsoever desirable for any religious organisation, can certainly not be a political agenda of any political party operating within secular framework of our Constitution of which secularism is the fundamental structure. It is Supreme Court judgement in Golaknath case that secularism is fundamental structure of the Constitution which cannot be changed even by another Constituent Assembly.

The CD produced by the BJP (its denial carries no conviction as during its release function senior leaders like Tandon and even BJP president Rajnath Singh were allegedly present) for its U.P. election campaign once again proves convincingly that it is not a secular party and is basically anti-Muslim in character. It uses very derogatory words for Muslims saying therein they marry four wives and produce 35 *pillas*, a derogatory Hindi word for unwanted children.

The contents of the CD are highly surprising. The Sangh Parivar even otherwise has been regularly propagating that Muslims marry four wives and produces 25 children (its campaign puts it as *ham panch, hamare pacchis* – we five our twenty five). Vishwa Hindu Parishad had taken out *Ekatma Yatra* in 1985 across the country and during this *Yatra* had distributed hundreds of thousands of such pamphlets.

How absurd is this propaganda that every Muslim marries four wives when the male-female ratio in our country is 935 female for 1000 male. And central Government survey conducted in 1997 shows that Muslims are at the bottom of those who practice polygamy. Muslims practicing bigamy or polygamy are just 5.2% whereas 5.8% upper caste Hindus Practice bigamy or polygamy. The tribals, dalits and Jains constitute even higher percentage of bigamous or polygamous marriage.

It is also wrong that no Muslim practices family planning and produces host of children. In 14 states family planning among Muslims is higher than that of Hindus. In Kerala family planning among Muslims is 64% as against just 35% among Hindus in U.P. In Pondicherry too family planning among Muslims is of the order of 85 per cent. This kind of cheap propaganda that Muslims marry four wives and produce 35 children does not behove an all India political party which aspires to come to power at the Centre.

Also, BJP claims to be most patriotic of all other parties. How can BJP be patriotic when it hates the largest minority of the country which is nearly 140 million in number? Mr. Narendra Modi, Chief Minister of Gujarat always talks of five crores of Gujaratis' *asmita* and makes it absolutely difficult for Muslims to live life of dignity and security. Even today Muslims in Gujarat are living as secondary citizens and most of the villages in Gujarat declare proudly 'you are welcome in village...in Hindu Rashtra.

It is unfortunate that even Union Government has never taken notice of such sign boards in hundreds of Gujarat villages. And on top of this Rajasthan text book of 12th standard tells its students that fascism is better than democracy as under fascism leader can take right decisions while in democracy it is not possible. It is also well known that the Sangh Parivar, particularly the RSS admires Hitler.

And one knows what relations exist between the RSS and BJP. BJP cannot defy any of the RSS dictates. Who knows this better than Mr. L.K. Advani who was removed as president of BJP just because he expressed his opinion about Jinnah in Pakistan. Do we need any more proofs for declaring BJP as non-secular, approving of fascism and targeting minorities? Can our democratic secular political culture allow such party to function within the parameters of our Constitution?

It is high time the Election Commission takes serious notice of all this and takes appropriate action under the People's Representation Act so that our democratic and secular culture remains unpolluted.

4

Hasrat Mohani – a Forgotten Freedom Fighter

We are celebrating 150 years of our first war of independence this year. All communities in India, Hindus, Muslims and others not only took part in this war but also made supreme sacrifices for this cause. This war of independence created unprecedented unity between people of India from top to bottom, from ruling classes to common people. All united to mount greatest challenge to the British rule in India.

Not only that Muslims played frontal role in this fight they also paid heavy price as the British wrath descended mainly on them. From emperor to ordinary peasants to Ulama were severely punished for taking part in 'mutiny' as the British chose to call it. The Muslim Zamindars lost their *jagirs* (landed estates) and large number of Ulama were exiled to places like Malta (an island near Italy) and Andaman Nicobar. Most eminent 'alim (theologian) of his time like Maulana Fazal Khairabadi was exiled to Andman where he died just before order for his release was received by the authorities.

In this line of eminent scholars, intellectuals and litterateur was Hasrat Mohani who was a great uncompromising freedom fighter from early twentieth century. He was graduate from Anglo Mohammedan Oriental (AMO) College, Aligarh, founded by Sir Syed. Hasrat Mohani was an eminent poet who used Ghazal poetry – a purely genre of love poetry – for political subjects and gave it a new turn. His contribution to Urdu Ghazal poetry was also of great significance. However, here we are mainly concerned with his role in freedom movement.

Hasrat Mohani (he is called Mohani as he was from Mohan in U.P.) was great freedom lover and never accepted British rule over India. He was great admirer of Lokmanya Tilak as he said 'freedom is my birth right' and always used to refer to him as Tilak Maharaj, even in his poetry. It is important to note that even his wife Nishatunnisa Begum, a woman who had always lived in purdah, also participated in freedom movement along with her husband.

He was so absorbed in the freedom movement that he became totally in different to any suffering, pain or pleasure. He maintained equanimity in all conditions. He could live on very little income or sometime no income at all. He was repeatedly jailed by the British but never complained about his imprisonment. His greatest quality was that whatever he thought was true will say it without any fear of consequences. He was totally uncompromising in that.

He never went back on his word. Once he published an article in his magazine. The writer had requested anonymity. The article was against the British rule. The authorities demanded from Hasrat the name of the writer. He refused. The British authorities threatened to confiscate security deposit and stop his publication. Hasrat still refused to disclose the name and not only his security deposit was confiscated, he was arrested, his precious library was destroyed and he was put in jail. But he refused to disclose the name of the writer of the article.

Maulana Hasrat Mohani was a very orthodox Muslim but at the same time he was also a communist. He used to call himself in his ghazal verse as 'Sufi Mu'min' and 'ishtraki Muslim' (a Sufi believer and a communist Muslim). He was one of the founders of Communist Party of India in 1925. He had great sympathy for workers and used to say Islam is very close to Soviet Communism. He even maintained that the word 'soviet' is from Arabic '*saviyyat*' which means equality. Islam's fundamental principle is equality and communism also stand for equality.

When the Indian National Congress held its session in Kanpur in 1925, Hasrat and his wife Nishatunnisa Begum came to the Congress *Pandal* with a procession of workers and peasants and wanted to enter into the *Pandal* but were stopped by Sevadal volunteers led by Jawaherlal Nehru. Nehru asked Seva Dal volunteer to *lathi* charge them. Begum Hasrat was furious and slapped Nehru and scolded him for such dictatorial order. Nehru realized his mistake and apologized to Begum Hasrat.

Begum Nishatunnisa herself was a great freedom fighter and stood firmly with her husband. A Muslim women from orthodox background played such dynamic and important role in freedom movement in early 20th century is really very refreshing and goes against the stereotype about Muslim women imprisoned in four walls and stepping out only wrapped in Purdah. Nishatunnisa was bold enough to confront even great personality like Pandit Nehru and scold him for stopping workers and peasants from entering into the Congress Pandal.

Maulana Hasrat Mohani was involved in freedom movement right from his college days and constantly faced problems during his college days for his uncompromising attitude. After coming out of college he started apparently an Urdu literary magazine called *Urdu-e-Moalla* but, as pointed out before, used to publish articles of political nature supporting freedom struggle.

He joined the Indian National Congress in 1904 and continued to participate in its session as a delegate until 1907 (Surat session). He also used to publish the reports of various Congress sessions like Calcutta, Benaras, Bombay etc. in his *Urdu-e-Moalla*. But in the Congress session of Surat in 1907 there was confrontation between *naram dal* (those who advocated soft approach) and *garam dal* (those who supported total freedom) Hasrat left Congress along with Tilak and he began hating the Congress as much as he hated the Muslim League which had come into existence and comprised of feudal elements and was loyal to the British government.

Hasrat remained great advocate of *garam dal* after leaving the Congress and published articles in support of it in his magazine and argued that the only destiny of Indian subcontinent is complete freedom from British imperialism. He continued to admire Lokmanya Tilak and his advocacy of complete freedom until Tilak's death. Maulana was also believer in struggle for freedom and said that any freedom given as a gift does not last for long.

Maulana never accepted pro-British stance of Muslim League. He severely criticized it in his articles in *Urdu-e-Moalla*. The Muslim league leaders used to highly praise the British government and what it is doing for Indians. On this he wrote an article in his magazine saying it is not necessary to thank the British for some incidental and temporary benefits accruing to Indians. He maintained that real thing is to judge what is intention of the British rulers. He was challenging the speech of Nawab Waqarul Mulk in this article as the Nawab had praised the British government for what it was doing for the Indian people.

It is interesting to note that Maulana Hasrat Mohani participated in the congress session in Ahmedabad in 1921 and moved resolution for complete freedom for India whereas Gandhiji was yet not prepared for it and was talking of Home Rule under the British supremacy. However, Hasrat did not succeed in view of Gandhiji's influence and his resolution was rejected. Muslim league session also had taken place in Ahmedabad simultaneously.

Maulana Hasrat addressed the Muslim League session as its president and spoke about complete freedom with enthusiasm but there too he did not succeed. Gandhiji referred to this in *Young India* and said that Hasrat did not succeed in his attempt for full freedom both from the Congress and Muslim League platform. Hasrat in his Muslim League address also proposed that we should establish United States in India on the lines of United States of America and give maximum rights to federating unit so that Muslims will also enjoy maximum autonomy in Muslim majority provinces. Thus the Maulana foresaw the later Cabinet Mission Plan proposed by the British Cabinet Mission in 1946 which could have saved partition of India.

Hasrat Mohani had proposed similar resolution in the Muslim League session of 1937 in which on one hand he proposed that the aim of Muslim League would be complete freedom from India and would strive to set up a democratic federation of India whose constitution will give full guaranteed to safeguard rights of minorities and their welfare. Thus even from the Muslim league platform also the Maulana continued to advocate complete freedom and a democratic and secular set up for India.

Hasrat Mohani also started a Swedeshi store in Aligarh to support the civil disobedience movement of early twenties.

He started this store when his magazine was confiscated by the British and Hasarat was such great supporter of Swedeshi that he even refused to use a foreign blanket in a cold December night when he had to sleep in Suleman Nadvi's office. Maulana Suleman Nadvi himself has narrated this event. Hasrat Mohani spent whole night shivering but did not use the blanket.

He was very diligent in observing all Islamic rites and used to fast during Ramadan in Jail when he had to grind one mound of grain every day in the month of May. But at the same time he was very active in the Communist movement and played very important role in founding the Communist Party in 1925. Such was the multifaceted personality of Maulana Hasrat Mohani who lived and died for freedom of India and a just social order in independent India. New generation should draw inspiration from his personality.

5

Attack on Taslima- Love of Islam or Love of Power?

It was shocking that three MLAs of Ittahidul Muslimin in Hyderabad gatecrashed into the book release function of her book *Lajjai* translated into Telugu on 9th August and tried to beat up Taslima and shouted slogans using unbecoming words, even using abusing language. And all this in the name of Islam as if Islam stands for such hooliganism.

The party leadership instead of condemning such wayward behaviour, approved of it and patted them on back. They were even given hero's welcome. One MLA even said that if Taslima comes to Hyderabad again, she will be beheaded. If elected representatives take law into their own hands, there cannot be greater tragedy. If they had done it without invoking Islam, it would have been a different story, though equally condemnable.

Was this for love of Islam? No way. It was love of power, pure and simple. The Party leadership thought it is good opportunity to strengthen and widen its electoral base. Human behaviour, especially political behaviour is extremely complex. Politicians, while acting in self-interest, invoke high ideals in order to cover up their utterly selfish motives.

Someone Imam even declared from Calcutta that he would pay Rs.50,000/- if anyone blackens Taslima's face. An Imam is supposed to be very respectable and responsible person who leads people in *namaz* (prayer) but also leads them in social and political matters. An Imam's behaviour should be highly restrained and responsible. I totally disagree with Taslima's views and think she is completely ignorant about Qur'anic teachings but that does not give anyone right to violently attack her or incite people to attack her.

Apart from the fact that such hooliganism is morally reprehensible it is unwise from the viewpoint of those who are opposed to Taslima's attacks on Islam. This gives her much more publicity that she deserves. Now this attack that took place in Hyderabad will give her worldwide publicity on one hand, and would make her celebrity in the eyes of those who are already hostile to Islam. Now reams and reams of papers will be blackened in her praise.

She would also be now much more hostile to Islam than ever before. She would really hate Islam because of hooliganism of some members of Ittihadul Muslimin. If we really love Islam than we should try to win her heart and soul through love and compassion. And that is what the Prophet of Islam did. It is well known story that a Jewish woman who hated the Prophet (PBUH) used to throw garbage on him whenever he passed from below her house. Once when she did not throw garbage on him, he inquired why she did not and was told she is sick. He immediately went to inquire about her health. She was so moved that immediately accepted Islam then and there.

What a contrast! Those who claim to love Prophet and Islam are attacking a woman and making her hate Islam more than before. This is madness, not wise behaviour and must be condemned as strongly as possible. These MLAs and crowd accompanied them have brought utter shame to Islam and Muslims. It is heartening that many religious leaders of Muslims and intellectuals have condemned it. Maulana Mustaqim of Jamiat –ul-Ulama-i-Hind, Shiah leader Maulana Ather Abbas Rizvi and several others have strongly condemned attack on Taslima Nasreen.

The book which was being released in Hyderabad had nothing to do with Islam. It was Telugu translation of her book on persecution of Hindu minority in Bangla Desh. After demolition of Babri Masjid like hooligans of Hindutva attacked Muslims all over India and engineered communal violence in number of cities and killed Muslims, the hooligans of Jamat-e-Islami of Bangla Desh attacked Hindus and demolished their temples and set fire to their houses. In *Lajja* (shame) she has condemned all this. Do we Muslims not heave sigh of relief when some fair-minded Hindus stand by Muslims when Hindu communal forces attack us? Should we not stand by fair-minded Muslims of Bangla Desh if they stand by Hindu minority?

It is true Taslima has written provocative articles on Islam. We must counter it by arguing on the basis of Qur'an rather than attacking her physically, and in very dignified language befitting a true Muslim. No one can cite a single verse of Qur'an or any hadith to support violence against others, even enemies, as long as they are peaceful. On the other hand we can cite several verses from the Qur'an, to support dignified behaviour.

The Qur'an says, " Call to the way of thy Lord with wisdom and goodly exhortation, and argue with them in the best manner" (16:125). Again what a contrast –the hooligans of Ittihadul Muslimin beat up a woman and other journalists and others present there. Also, Allah says in the Qur'an "..do not be aggressors, Allah does not love aggressors." (2:190). And even if a Muslim renounces Islam and becomes unbeliever, no one has right to punish him/her except Allah.

"Those who believe", says Qur'an, "then disbelieve, again believe and again disbelieve, then increase in disbelief, Allah is not referring to any punishment for those who repeatedly believe and disbelieve and increase in disbelief, let alone human beings punishing them of their own. Even if Taslima has ceased to believe and has increased in her disbelief, no one has any right among human beings to punish her. It is matter of her conscience. All one can do is to dialogue with her in dignified way and then leave it to her conscience.

II

Democracies in socially backward countries like India face an acute dilemma. The entire functioning of democracy depends on rights of people and freedom of conscience and right to believe or disbelieve. Both individual and collective rights are sacred in democracy. However, politicians greedy for votes of illiterate masses, and even educated middle class people, try to incite religious feelings and get their votes. Most of the politicians find this easy way to legislative assemblies or Parliament. They emerge as champions of this or that religion and grab their votes.

This is what the Sangh Parivar did by launching an aggressive movement for Ramjanambhoomi and demolished Babri Masjid and took pride in that act of lawlessness and destruction. The Sangh leaders launched not only aggressive campaign but Sangh leaders like Uma Bharti and Sadhvi Rithambara used abusive language against Muslims and the Government did nothing. They allowed hate campaign to go on.

If the authorities had taken stiff action against Uma Bharti and Rithambara, it would have sent a strong signal to all others that they cannot get away with such aggressive campaigns against all norms of democracy. Democracy cannot succeed without following rule of law. If Uma Bharti and Rithambara had been punished, MLAs of Ittihadul Muslimin would not have dared to indulge in this hooliganism.

However, as the Swedish scholar who wrote *Asian Drama* observed India's is the soft government and refuses to act until all damage is done. Taslima Nasreen's attackers also got away with symbolic arrest and were released on bail immediately thereafter. It speaks volumes about our indifferent approach and also fear of votes.

So many communal riots take place because no guilty in the riots is ever punished. All of them know this and have nothing to care for consequences. And riots keep on taking place. Mumbai riots more than 800 persons were killed, many of them most brutally, and yet state is extremely reluctant to act lest Shiv Sena may not approve of it. Can this ever be the reason for not acting at all for a democratic government?

This is indeed bad omen for Indian democracy. The people involved in such public crimes must be severely punished to send strong message that hooliganism will not be tolerated in any case. Rule of law must be applied under any circumstances. Politicians should not be allowed to incite people publicly to indulge in mayhem and murder. This is repeatedly happening in our democracy.

It is heartening sign that many religious personalities among Muslims and secular intellectuals among them have come out strongly condemning this attack on Taslima Nasreen. Still many columnists, even waiting for a day started demanding where are those Muslims and secularists who immediately condemn Hindutvawadis but keep quiet when some Muslim fanatics indulge in such extremist action. Many such columnists will come out with many such articles and further aggravate feelings in majority community.

We are not a mature democracy and should come out against any act of hooliganism and violence whosoever perpetrates it, Hindus, Muslims, Sikhs or Christians. We must promote zero tolerance towards any act of violence. It should be our litmus test. If we want to enjoy fruits of secular democracy we must shed all forms of partisan feelings. Politicisation of religion in our democracy has already done enough damage. How much more damage we want to inflict?

Is any one listening?

6

Communal Riots 2007

Every year we monitor communal riots in India. Here is the account of riots, which took place in 2007, which we could monitor through various sources. The first minor riot took place in Bandi district, near Jaipur in Rajasthan on 18th January. Five persons were injured and 7 shops were set to fire when riot broke out when persons belonging to Muslims entered a Gym about which there was controversy and fight broke out between persons belonging to two communities. Of the 5 persons injured one was a policeman and 7 shops burnt resulted in huge economic loss. Police brought the rioting under control and curfew was imposed.

Indore in M.P. has become another sensitive area where communal violence breaks out of and on 21st January clashes broke out between workers of BJP and minority community and this trouble began after some people belonging to minority community showed swords to a BJP office bearer. Several people were injured in Mukripura where rioting broke out and a motorcycle was set afire. Police officer Anshuman Yadav said that situation was brought under control and police had to use teargas shells to disperse mob. There was tension in the whole city.

Bangalore saw outbreak of communal violence on 21st January two days after Muslims had demonstrated on Friday against hanging of Saddam Husain in Iraq. Police fired and in Shivajinagar area one person died and 3 were injured. In fact before this rally there was communal tension and there was incident of stoning in which 50 persons were injured. Then the Hindu Virat Mahasabha took out *Shobha Yatra* on the occasion of 100th birth centenary of Guru Golwalkar and the yatris set several places on fire. The police fired in which one man was killed and a police constable was stabbed. Other 4 police officials were also injured. About 20 civilians were also injured. The violent mob set five buses and several cars to fire. Many shops belonging to Muslims were also set ablaze.

Next it was turn of Gorakhpur, U.P. where on the occasion of Muharram on 27th January (on 7th Muharram procession) there was stoning from some houses in Khotipura area. About a dozen persons were injured in stoning from both sides. The violent mob set fire to one Mazar (shrine) and one car. Curfew was imposed in three areas. Communal tension erupted after one person Agarhari was killed in firing by some unknown person.

However, Gorakhpur continued to burn for couple of days more. Violence again broke out on 29th January when the BJP M.P. Yogi Adityanath was arrested for provoking violence. The demonstrators set ablaze three jeeps and several commercial establishments. The Government of U.P. suspended District Magistrate and S.P. for failing to control communal violence. One person had died and several injured in communal violence and so curfew was imposed in three areas. In fact violence continued as Adityanath is known for provoking communal violence. The Central Government had to think of sending central forces to control violence. Sriprakash Jaiswal, Minister of State for Home in the Centre said this after touring riot affected areas of Gorakhpur.

Next communal incident broke out in Beawar town of Rajgarh district, M.P. On 1st February fight broke out between two communities when some posters about a programme were torn and this became cause of violence. There was intense fighting between members of two communities. Several shops and cars were set to fire. Then curfew was imposed and orders were issued to fire on any one violating curfew. The administration also imposed ban on all politicians from entering the area. About 40 persons were arrested for indulging in violence.

Indore again witnessed communal violence on 12th February. The violence broke out when it was rumoured that a Muslim youth beat a Hindu girl. Soon crowds gathered and violent incidents began. Several vehicles were burnt and 10 persons were injured. Violence was so intense that police had to fire in the air and curfew was imposed in three police station areas.

There were minor clashes in Jaipur on 16th February in *Lodon ki Gali* in Jaipur city of Rajasthan when a Muslim threw chicken waste in a gutter and the Hindus raised hue and cry and stoning started in which 10 persons were injured. Police arrested 10 persons. Police also arranged a meeting of the elders of the two communities for peace, which had salutary effect.

Another incident of communal violence occurred in Aliganj area of Sultanpur when some boys of majority community indulged in eve teasing and used unbecoming language against some girls going to a photo studio. When this news spread in no time people from both the communities gathered and began stoning each other. Many persons were injured of which two persons, one Hindu and one Muslim were critical and several vehicles were set ablaze. Some firing also took place from both sides.

Darbhanga in Bihar witnessed communal violence due to desecration of one grave belonging to Muslim community. 12 persons were injured. Similarly communal violence broke out in Chittorgarh District at Begin Tehsil on 18th March because some processionists threw gulal on a mosque. Police arrested 70 persons. Thus violence was controlled.

Poonch in Jammu part of J&K witnessed communal violence when 1000 strong group of Muslims occupied a plot of land belonging to a BJP leader and constructed a mosque. The incident occurred on 24th March. The police intervened and stopped construction of mosque. Next day people again began to construct mosque and then riots broke out injuring 20 people when police stopped them and demolished the incomplete structure. Over 25 people many of them policemen were injured in pitched battles between police and rioters. As tension mounted police imposed curfew and sealed off all approach roads and shut down the local telephone exchange. As violence continued army was called in and construction of mosque was stopped.

On 28th March there was trouble in Lalgaon, 40 kms from Jamnagar, in Gujarat when a girl participant in a Ramnaumi procession was teased. The processionists were provoked and stoning started. The mob set fire to the house and shop of the teaser. The police had to lathicharge the mob. The police then arrested the youth who had teased the girl and police bandobast was made in the town.

Madhya Pradesh (M.P.) has become highly communal violence prone since BJP has come to power there. On April 1 again there was communal violence in Narsinghgadh town of Rajgarh district when two processions Hanuman Jayanti and

Miladun Nabi procession were being taken out. The processionists of Hanuman Jayanti stopped near a mosque and began shouting anti-Muslim slogans, a police official said. It was also reported that one person died but it could not be ascertained whether it was riot related death. To control the situation five additional companies of SAF, RAF and STF were rushed to Narshinghgadh. Police also had to fire and use teargas shells to disperse unruly mobs of the two communities.

Later three bodies were discovered killed in communal violence. More than 100 persons were arrested and illegal weapons seized in raids. Two bodies were discovered in a pond and one person died as a teargas shell hit him. The analysts said that these riots are clear sign of BJP's poll preparations. The party, it is said, is out to repeat Gujarat experiment.

On 12th April Umarkhed, in Nander district, Maharashtra witnessed communal violence. A Muslim youth Zamir was murdered by some unknown persons and when his funeral procession was being taken out some people in the procession burnt a travel bus. Then a Shiv Sena leader summoned Shiv Sainiks and Bajrang Dal activists and began looting and burning hundreds of shops. Police arrested many miscreants looting and burning shops. Some Muslim youth also then retaliated and both sides suffered losses worth lakhs of rupees. To control the situation additional police forces were summoned.

Shahjahanpur, M.P. witnessed communal violence on 13th May in which 6 persons were injured including 3 women. It was told by police authorities that violence broke out when two buses carrying marriage parties belonging to two communities clashed on the question of giving way to the bus. Police reached on the spot and separated two fighting groups.

Ahmedabad the communally most sensitive city saw minor clashes between Hindus and Muslims on 14th June when a truck carrying mutton was stoned by miscreants. Soon members of both the communities began stoning each other in which 18 persons were injured. However, police intervened and controlled situation.

On August 14 Tenkasi town known for fireworks manufacturing witnessed communal violence in which 6 persons were killed. The violence broke out on the question of constructing mosque opposite a temple. There was old enmity between two groups. A year before Hindu Munnani leader Kumar Pandian was stabbed to death allegedly by members of Tamil Nadu Muslim Munnetra Kazhagam. Munnani activists retaliated by stabbing TMMK leader Sait Khan who survived. Thus situation was simmering and clashes occurred in the market place and six persons were killed.

Next communal violence took place on 31st August when two groups belonging to two communities clashed after a college girl complained that she was teased. It was again a case of girl teasing which led to eruption on August 31. A college student of Shahera village complained to her community members that she was being harassed. A couple of boys belonging to the other community. Members of both communities gathered and indulged in stone throwing at each other. A local police fired a round in the air and lobbed tear gas shells to disperse the crowd. The crowd had turned violent and burnt four vehicles and shouted slogans against each other. The police, fearing worst, even called additional forces. However, situation came under control.

Next on 1st September Allahabad witnessed communal flare up when Qur'an was desecrated in Kareli area. Some pages of Qur'an were found burnt in an old cemetery of Kareli area. The news spread like wild fire and thousands of people gathered and began shouting slogans and began stoning. Police vehicles were damaged due to stoning. In Kareli area 80% are Muslims. Since people gathered were shouting slogan in support of

Samajwadi M.P. Atiq Ahmed, BJP believed it was done by followers of Atiq Ahmed. The police fired in the air and lobbed teargas shells to disperse the mob. Fourteen persons were arrested. Curfew was imposed in five police station areas.

Then it was turn in Jalgaon in Maharashtra to go through communal bout on 17th September when some Muslim youth tried to stop a Ganesh procession which was passing through an unauthorized route and hell was let loose. The police rushed to the spot and faced shower of stones. Several police people were injured and had to be hospitalized. It must be said that the police showed great deal of patience and did not react to the mob violence otherwise whole Jalgaon would have burnt. The mob could be mollified only after police announced that 20 persons who allegedly obstructed Ganesh procession have been arrested. The situation was saved.

On September 19 Surat experienced communal violence when a VHP leader of Gauraksha samiti (Cow protection committee) was murdered allegedly by a Muslim. The family of VHP leader alleged that police has given shelter to the murderer and refused to perform his last rites. One person was stabbed and four shops burnt as fresh violence erupted by an irate mob in Kosadi village in Surat district. Jashubhai Darbar, VHP leader was maintaining vigil against illegal slaughter of cows and he was attacked by a mob with swords and iron rods and died on spot. As news of murder spread, Hindus from nearby villages gathered and targeted Muslim establishments and houses. One person was stabbed in Kim village. Police arrested 30 persons in connection with rioting in Kosadi village. There is 5000 Muslim population in Kosadi and it is alleged cow slaughter is rampant in the area.

Panigate area of Baroda city is highly sensitive area and it witnessed frequent riots. On 22nd September it erupted in communal violence on the occasion of Ganapati procession.

Tension built up as on Friday the Ganapati processionists halted before a mosque and began dancing and singing in a obscene manner. Then stoning started on the procession and riots broke out. The police commissioner P.C.Thaker himself was injured in stoning. Many others were also injured in rioting. Even 30 policemen including a deputy police commissioner were injured. A rumour was spread that a Bajrang Dal activist was killed and rioting spread in other areas of Baroda. Police commissioner said that he would take action against those who spread this rumor.

Baroda again witnessed communal violence on 27th September again on the occasion of Ganapati Visarjan (immersion) in which 10 persons were injured However, police controlled the situation in time.

On 28 September Khamgaon, in Maharashtra came under the spell of communal violence on the occasion of Ganesh procession. Three processions passed off peacefully through Aman Chowk. But the fourth procession accompanied by local MLA stopped before a mosque and indulged in provocative acts. Some Muslims requested the procession to go ahead as it was Iftar time (breaking fast). Then stoning on procession started though some maintain miscreants themselves organized stoning. Then riots broke out and police played a partisan role. Next day also in some areas Hindus attacked Muslim houses and there was police firing in which one Muslim youth was injured. Police role was quite pro-rioters of Hindu community. It is alleged that thousands of Hindus attacked Barde plot and Yasinkhan plot (Muslim mohallas) right in presence of police. The mob openly used obscene words against Muslim women. Curfew had to be imposed in Khamgaon. Shiv Sena members even threatened Muslims publicly that 'you observe Ramzan, we will celebrate Eid'. And despite all this innocent Muslims were arrested. A high level inquiry was demanded by Muslims of Khamgaon in the role of police and those responsible for riots.

On 7th October Communal violence broke out in Jaisalmer, border town in Rajasthan. The Hindutva forces have penetrated even in border areas now. The violence took place on the issue of cow slaughter. Sangh Parivar gave call for bandh and it resulted in violence in which mob set ablaze 8 houses and two vehicles belonging to minority community.

We witnessed communal violence next in Amravati, another communally sensitive town in Maharashtra. On 22nd October Hindus and Muslims clashed in which 26 people were injured. The clash occurred during Durga immersion procession. The clashes took place in Achalpur of Amravati district. The mob set fire to several jewellery shops and police had to resort to firing. It all began with some youngsters dancing and throwing gulal which fell on religious place and two groups clashed and stoning and incidents of arson started. Achalpur had not witnessed communal violence on this scale. Violence spread to several areas and jewellery market was looted and burnt. Police fired at least 50 rounds to disperse the rioting mob. An indefinite curfew was imposed. Achalpur is a historical town once ruled by Bahmani rulers. It was a devastating scene after rioting. Here too police played partisan role and a Muslim delegation met R.R.Patil, Home Minister of Maharashtra in this connection and told him that one policeman was involved in raping a Muslim woman. Many Muslims fled from Achalpur for fear of their lives. Kadre, a police inspector was subsequently suspended.

Savner town in Indore district came under spell of communal violence on 3rd November where a bye-election for assembly seat was due. Violence broke out after some altercation on a teashop. One person was killed according to official sources but media reported three dead and several injured. Curfew had to be imposed. Some analysts maintained that this riot was part of a conspiracy since assembly election was due on 12th December. According to a Milli Gazette report Police and SRP men were among the rioters in looting and burning 137 shops burnt, property worth crores of rupees were destroyed and more than 200 persons arrested.

On Christmas Day i.e. on 25th December riots broke out against Christians in Kandhamal district. This was first time that Christians faced systematic riots in which VHP was deeply involved. Several churches were burnt and according to official account 4 persons died but unofficially 12 persons died. Orrisa has been the centre of anti-Christian violence. It was in this state that an Australian priest working among the lepers Graham Stains was burnt alive along with his two sons. BJP and VHP have become very bold since BJP is part of ruling coalition. Though Christians face charge of conversion everywhere by Sangh Parivar but Orissa has large tribal population and VHP has made it centre of its anti-Christian activities. So far churches were burnt, priests attacked and nuns molested in several parts of India, specially in tribal areas but Orissa witnessed full fledged communal riots for the first time. This naturally came as a great shock for the Christian community.

Conclusion

We have given above account of communal riots throughout 2007 which we could monitor. May be some riots may have been left out which were very minor in character. It is our efforts to monitor almost all riots which take place in India. Most of the riots listed here are small in character. The causes, it will be seen, are very petty. In no other countries such petty causes will result in communal violence. Personal disputes soon acquire communal character.

This is of course result of widespread communal propaganda and law taking no serious notice of communal organizations. No action is ever taken against provocative newspaper articles or speeches by political leaders. Everyone thinks of nothing but votes and no one cares for the country and woes of the people. Even no concerted efforts are made to secularise police. Several RSS trained persons join police force and they show sympathy with majority community rioters.

Communal forces are aggressively exploiting religion for political ends and it appears there is silent consensus among all political parties (except of course left parties) including secular parties like Congress, Samajwadi Party, Mayawati's BSP, Janta Dal (U) as well as Janta Dal (secular) to use communal sentiments for political purposes. Some symbolic noises are made against communalism but except left all want to benefit from religious and caste sentiments. It is dangerous game and very harmful to unity of the country in the long run. But who cares if you can capture power today?

7

Secularism and its Problems in India

It will be no exaggeration if I say secularism is the very life breath of Indian politics. One can hardly conceive of Indian polity sans secularism. However, it also faces several problems in Indian context. We will throw light and discuss the problematic of secularism in India. Before we do so we must explain meaning and context of Indian secularism.

Secularism in India did not emerge, unlike in Europe, as a result of struggle against authority of church. In Europe since it emerged as a result of struggle against Church, it carried within itself an atheistic trend. It certainly implied a sort of indifference towards religion, if not antagonism to it. Recently this has been further intensified due to increasing consumerism and materialism.

In India religion has always been at the centre stage. Thus secularism here was never conceived as indifference, much less antagonism, to religion. Secularism was conceived as a philosophy giving equal respect to all religions including regional faith traditions. When Indian National Congress was founded, its founders feared it may be dubbed as a Hindu party by non-Hindu minorities. Thus it was sought to be made an all inclusive party and three of its presidents came from minority communities in its early days: 1) Badruddin Tyebji from Bombay; 2) W.C.Banerjee– A Christian from Bengal and Dadabhai Nawroji from Parsi Community.

Thus the Congress got support from all these communities from the day one. Even the 'Ulama, who were struggling against British rule readily supported it and urged their fellow-Muslims to join the Congress *en mass*. Maulana Qasim Ahmed Nanotwi, the founder of Darul 'Ulum Deoband, issued a fatwa to this effect himself and collected several more such fatwas from other 'ulama of repute and published them under the title of *Nusrat-ul-Ahrar* (Help for the Freedom fighters). The 'Ulama were convinced of the all inclusive character of the Congress Party and enthusiastically cooperated with it for throwing out British imperialist from India.

Thus our secularism is more in multi-religious context than any struggle against church or any religious authority for that matter. The Congress adopted secularism as an all-inclusive philosophy. Our country has a very rich experience of religious pluralism and multi-culturalism for centuries. We were never mono-religious or mono-cultural in any period of our history. The West has known religious pluralism and multi-culturalism only after IInd World War.

Some intellectuals immediately after independence thought secularism in India also should mean indifference to religion, if not being anti-religious and criticized state for associating with any religious events. Even our first Prime Minister Jawaharlal Nehru was more or less of this view. But soon he had realized that it may not be workable in India and defined Indian secularism as equal protection to all religions by state. Thus real criteria for state remaining secular is whether it provides equal support to all religions or inclines more towards one or the other religion.

Having thrown light on the nature of Indian secularism we come to the problems Indian secularism faces. In fact we can divide state into two categories: 1) notional and 2) functional. As far as notional aspect is concerned it is defined by its Constitution. The Indian state adopted the Constitution which defines nature and functions of state, rights citizens enjoy and role of executive and judiciary.

As far as notional aspect is concerned i.e. constitutional provisions, I do not think there is much of a problem. When we faced some problems the Constitution was amended and our Constitution has been amended more than 100 times. Thus as far as notional aspect is concerned there is no problem. But its functional aspect is expressed through the government and its way of functioning.

The problematic of secularism starts with functional aspect, not with its notional aspect. The government is formed by a political party. For more or less 10 years after independence the Congress continued to rule and under Nehru Congress remained firmly committed to secularism but even under Nehru, it faced severe problems as other congress leaders were not so categorically committed and had quite ambiguous and some of them even communally inclined attitude.

Thus in 1948 itself Chief Minister of U.P. Govind Ballabh Pant, defied Nehru's instructions and did not remove idols of Ram and Sita which were installed in Babri masjid at midnight. Even Sardar Patel had written to C.M. of U.P. to remove the idols. If Pant had taken the step India would not have faced such huge problem in late eighties and early nineties.

Indian state, functionally, always remained soft as so clearly demonstrated by Jan Myrdal, a Swedish Economist, who wrote his famous work *Asian Drama* in sixties. The successive Governments kept on yielding to pressures and took decisions which did not conformed to secular values which our Constitution upholds. Even Nehru felt isolated on the question of curbing communal violence in Jabalpur which shook him.

On several crucial questions Central Government yielded to pressures and took unprincipled decisions violating secular values. There are several instances but two most crucial questions on which Government yielded which severely affected Indian secular polity, were Shah Bano judgment and the Babri masjid issue. Rajiv Gandhi bowed to the pressure by some Muslim leaders and enacted a law reversing the Supreme Court judgment in the Shah Bano case and Shri Narsimha Rao did nothing to save Babri masjid and let it be demolished by the BJP hooligans.

This reversal of Supreme Court judgment in one case and total and deliberate non-action to save Babri Masjid seriously compromised Indian secularism and it proved that Indian Government does not act firmly on secular principles but yields to all sorts of pressures and takes opportunist stand. It never wishes to send strong and principled message by taking firm stand on crucial matters and does not mind at all displaying its weakness and opportunism for the sake of power.

Another crucial issue is communal violence. India was repeatedly rocked by communal violence in post-independence period. The Congress leadership, it is said, ultimately agreed to partition to save country from civil war and curb widespread communal violence and hoped that independent India would not witness communal violence. That is why Nehru was greatly shaken by Jabalpur riots which he never expected in independent India.

But this was just the beginning. Had he been alive he would have witnessed much worse riots in 1969 in Ahmedabad (in which more than 1000 people were done to death brutally) and 1970 Bhivandi-Jalgaon riots (in which about 400 persons including women and children) were done to death. Then followed several major riots in eighties which were worse in severity. Some of these riots were Moradabad (1980), Biharsharif (1981), Baroda and Meerut (19820, Neili, Assam (1983) in which more than 4000 people were massacred, Bombay Bhivandi riots and anti-Sikh riots (1984 May and November), Meerut (1987), it was in Hashimpura, Meerut that 42 persons were pulled out of their houses and shot by PAC and their bodies thrown into canal, 1989 Bhagalpur riots in which more than 800 persons perished and then 1992-93 riots in Mumbai, Surat, Ahmedabad, Bhopal, Kanpur and several other places in India.

Now all these riots took place under Congress regimes, both at the Centre and states. These were, to say the least, horrible riots and Congress regime never tried to curb communal violence seriously. Not because the Congress party swerved from secular ideology but because most of the individual Congressmen were of either communal bent of mind or truly secular individuals in the party felt helpless and isolated.

For all politicians be they of the Congress or any other secular parties, power was ultimate aim, not constitutional principles or secularism. If power is prioritized over principles, country would witness such calamities repeatedly. State machinery was always grossly misused in all major communal riots. The politicians used police to promote their own interests and seriously compromised integrity and professionalism of the police.

Police, with some honourable exceptions, always displayed its communal character in almost all the riots. In Bombay riots 1992-93 and Gujarat riots 2002 it played leading role and brought shame to itself. This is mostly because police was instrumental in promoting interests of politicians and so even honest policemen got isolated, transferred or demoted. Lower ranks of the police has been highly communalized and even brutalized.

The governments are quite unwilling to take steps to organize refresher courses for the police to instill in them secular values as they want to use them time and again to organize communal violence as and when it suits them. All election strategies are also based on caste and communal arithmetic and hence it is nearly impossible to be firm on secular values and principles. Our electoral method is exclusive, rather than inclusive. Parties aim at this or that caste and community votes. Thus elections are won by excluding some and including some.

As long as our electoral method is exclusivistic, secularism would continued to be weakened. We have to abandon first past the post method which tends to work by excluding one community or the other and opt for inclusive method by adopting 51 per cent votes compulsory for winning and then no politician would target one community excluding other community or caste. This will help greatly in promoting secularism which is about including all in political processes.

8

Multi-religious Democracy and its Challenges

Western pattern of democracy was evolved in mono-religious societies. Almost all European countries had mainly Christianity as the sole religion with sprinkling of Jews living in ghettoes having no franchise. Thus there were no challenges of living in multi-religious society. In India too, multi-religious society was not a problem for centuries and Indian society never saw any inter-religious tensions, let alone violence.

It was only when British rule was introduced based on policy of divide and rule followed by democratic measures involving competition between elites of two communities that resulted in not only inter-communal tensions but also division of the country. Challenges of multi-religious society are indeed grave, if governance is not based on principles and values and cooperation rather than competition.

The western countries also had to face these challenges in the post-colonial era. They termed it as multi-culturalism and pluralism. Though in principle they did accept pluralism and multi-culturalism but could not avoid inter-racial and inter-cultural tensions. Earlier racialism in the west was directed only against black Africans but in post-colonial society, against Indians and other coloured people also. And now it has emerged as anti-Islam and anti-Muslim also.

We in India simply imitated British model of parliamentary system though the British model was evolved in a mono-religious setting. The tensions emerged in its early stages itself. Communal riots in nineteenth century were result of not only British divide and rule but also of anti-communal rhetoric of indigenous political and religious elite. Even the Shuddhi and Tablighi movements reflected inter-communal hostilities. There were no such movements in pre-British Moghul period. The two communities enjoyed almost cordial relationship. What went wrong?

As soon as it became evident that British are going to introduce limited democracy the competition for power began and elites of the two communities began to make demands for more and more power in the name of their respective communities. Thus, in a way religious pluralism which was our strength all along, became our political weakness. Our politics was now based less on principles and values but more on vested interests of the two elites.

Also, there were other problems. Democracy in India did not evolve over a period of time along with de-feudalisation of society but as a result of introduction by the colonial rulers in a way that took interests of various groups into account. Thus very foundation of democracy in India in its early colonial period was flawed. In Western countries, on the other hand, it evolved over a period of time and as a result of long drawn struggle, be it in England or in France, or some other European countries.

But the leaders of freedom struggle like Mahatma Gandhi, Nehru and Abul Kalam Azad, studied the western model of democracy and principle and values on which it was based and adopted them to suit our conditions. They understood values of individual freedom and distancing state from religion and religious beliefs and hence realized the value of secularism in a multi-religious society.

But there were certain contradictions in those principles and our socio-religious reality. In western society as a result of long drawn struggle and as a result of industrialization and emergence of bourgeois class, individual freedom developed sound basis. But there was no such social basis in India for individual freedom. An individual in India is bound by many shackles and cannot easily break caste and communal bonds. It is also very difficult for him to break these bonds.

In India even today, after several decades of freedom he hardly makes individual decisions. He is more part of his caste or community and takes collective interests or collective pride into account while making political decisions. West had long overcome these obstacles to individual freedom.

Our constitution is based on individual, not on collective rights except in case of certain collective rights of minorities. These individual constitutional rights and collective bonds, often collide with each other producing caste and communal tensions or even violence. This is social basis of communalism in India. The politicians are well aware of this contradiction which they exploit to the maximum extent possible.

When elections are due politicians switch to caste and communal mode. Certain parties and individuals have 'perfected' this art. For example Bal Thackeray of Shiv Sena, Advani and Narendra Modi of BJP have become adept in exploiting communal sentiments. BJP through Advani and Narendra Modi apply Hindu rhetoric as Jinnah applied Islamic rhetoric in pre-partition days.

L.K.Advani evolved Ramjanambhoomi rhetoric to bring BJP to power by stirring Hindu sentiments among a large section of Hindus and Narendra Modi, evolved a Gujarat model of his own by provoking anti-Muslim pogrom in 2002 and getting two-third majority. In the current elections in Gujarat (2007 Assembly elections), he first raised developmental issues but switched on to communal rhetoric the moment he realized this may not ensure his victory.

Gujarat, under the leadership of Narendra Modi, has not only been completely polarized between Hindus and Muslims but is emerging as pro Fascist state. When communal rhetoric is stretched to its extreme, this danger is bound to emerge. Many political thinkers and analyst are pointing out it is moment of serious reflection for BJP itself. Narendra Modi, by using communal rhetoric to its extreme, has now emerged as the supreme leader, much larger than party itself.

News reports point out that he takes his own name almost once per minute throwing aside party and party programme. The BJP leaders encouraged him in his communal rhetoric and celebrated his 'new model' to win elections and now are paying for it. The BJP will find it very difficult to forestall Modi if he wins elections this time too. At least in Gujarat, BJP will be sidelined and Moditva, rather than Hindutva, will reign supreme.

In a parliamentary democracy, no leader can be allowed to emerge larger than life. Mahatma Gandhi, a great man by his deeds, also had humility to understand importance of principles of democracy and value of people's participation in political process. He did not project himself and his ego in politics as Narendra Modi is doing. Narendra Modi thinks he alone can save Gujarat, he alone can guarantee security of Hindu Gujaratis, he alone can ward off terrorism (by killing innocent people be it in communal violence or be it in fake encounters). No party, no principles, no ideology, is important.

Such a behaviour is totally destructive of all democratic values. Of course communal politics itself is destructive of all democratic principles. Example of Pakistan is also before us. It was founded on communal politics and could not find stability till today. It could not even remain united and fell apart in 1971. It is now experiencing increasing communal and sectarian violence and its rulers often cater to US interests, rather than those of Pakistan and Pakistani people.

Gujarat today appears to be counter-part of Pakistani politics in India. Mere elections make it democratic not. BJP, allowed Narendra Modi to win elections for it in Gujarat through mass murder in 2002. Now Narendra Modi is beyond party's control. He is trying to emerge on Gujarat political scene as a supreme. People wear his mask, people take only his name, and his supporters are hardly concerned with BJP or Party programme. His BJP colleagues are revolting against him and challenging him.

Narendra Modi Emerged as supreme only as a result of communal politics of BJP and more he oppresses minorities, more support he gathers. Even if Modi is defeated in this election (possibility of his defeat is there, but no certainty) there is no guarantee that he will be really cut to size. His image will remain larger than life among his supporters and believers. They will definitely work with greater zeal to see him again in power.

The main philosophy of democracy is that no leader can be larger than people. It is true we have sustained parliamentary democracy for six decades with short interruption (in the form of emergency) but we have still not developed democratic culture and democratic ethos. We cannot develop democratic ethos and democratic culture until we find proper balance between individual freedom on one hand, and, our collective identity, on the other. We are still swayed by collective identity at the cost of individual freedom. It is still very difficult to achieve this balance.

Mahatma Gandhi had very well understood this need for balanced between collective life and individual freedom and hence his emphasis on inter-religious harmony and democratic rights. Nehru and Azad too were not far behind and repeatedly talked about unity in diversity and understanding the value of working out this fine balance. Communal rhetoric appears very attractive to some politicians but nothing is more destructive of our country and society than this rhetoric.

9

Mainstreaming Minorities

I often confront a question in my workshops and lectures as to why Muslims do not want to become part of mainstream. In a way it is quite a hackneyed question but nevertheless it persists in the minds of many people, even among those who are quite secular. Before we discuss whether minorities, especially Muslims, are part of mainstream or not, we should have clear idea of what is mainstream.

To understand what is mainstream, important question is who defines mainstream? As the saying goes culture of the ruling class is the ruling culture, mainstream is also what the ruling or upper classes to be the mainstream. In democracy there should not be any question of ruling class but our democracy is hardly participatory, much less an ideal democracy. The idea of ruling class is very much the ruling idea in our democracy.

Thus what constitutes mainstream is mainly defined by the ruling classes, which ultimately means the upper caste and upper class people. For them mainstream is mainly constituted by those who follow classical culture of upper caste Hindus, are highly educated and enjoy certain reasonable standard of life. To be part of mainstream it is very necessary to be part of Vedic culture.

By this definition even dalits and tribals are hardly part of mainstream. They are also poor, uneducated and speak dialect, rather than Sanskritised Hindi or any other classical language. But only difference is that they are natives of India and do not follow ay 'foreign religion'. Also, they belong to 'other' castes but not to 'other' religion. Moreover, their otherisation will result in fragmentation of Hindu solidarity and thus their otherisation can be politically loosing proposition.

Thus though dalits and tribals are not part of national mainstream, silence about them is better part of political strategy. But otherisation of Muslims has been going on ever since the British rulers adopted the strategy of divide and rule and the communal forces found it quite useful after independence and through their propaganda the myth of Muslims, not being part of mainstream spread and some secular minded people also became victim of it. The myth needs to be examined critically.

First thing to note is that entire community should not be treated as single homogenised unit. Indian Muslim community is highly diverse, as diverse as the Hindu community. There is regional, cultural, linguistic and religious (sectarian) diversity besides economic diversity. How can one maintain that entire Muslim community is away from Indian mainstream?

Are Muslims of Kerala and Tamil Nadu who are firmly rooted in native cultures and speak Malayalam and Tamil respectively, not part of Indian mainstream? If they are not then even Malayalam and Tamil Hindus too, are not part of mainstream. Muslims, Christians and Hindus of these regions wear similar clothes, eat similar food, enjoy same music and follow same regional customs and traditions. More or less same applies to Andhra and Karnataka Muslims (with the exception of Hyderabad and few other towns).

What about Kashmiri Muslims and Pandits? Do they not speak same language and follow similar traditions? Kashmiri Muslims and Pandits are quite integrated. How can one maintain that Kashmiri Muslims are not part of mainstream whereas Hindus are? It will be quite untenable position. Then what about Kargil Muslims and Gujjar and Bakarwal tribes of Kashmir Valley? These Gujjar and Bakarwal Muslims have their own identity separate from Kashmiri Muslims and are firmly rooted in their tribal culture.

Then what about Muslims in rural areas of north India i.e. in U.P. and Bihar? They speak same dialect as rural Hindus, follow same customs and traditions and even wear same dress as Hindus of the region do. They speak Braj, Bhojpuri, Maithili, Rajasthani, Malvi and similar other dialects. Many of them go to mosques for prayers wearing *dhoti* and turban which is considered a 'Hindu dress'.

Also, what about Bohras, Khojas and Memons? They are so well rooted in Gujarat culture and they speak Gujarati or Kutcchi wherever they go in the world? Their entire culture is rooted in Gujarat or different regions of Gujarat. Will they also be considered as not being part of mainstream?

Then what about Parsis, Paswans, Weavers, Silawats (brick layers), Rangrez (dyers), Bangle-makers, Malis (vegetable and fruit sellers from Mahrashtra), Raeens (vegetable sellers from Bihar) and so on. Are they not Indians and part of Indian mainstream or just because they are low caste illiterate and uncultured, they cannot be part of Indian mainstream? Are then their counterpart Hindu low caste dalits and backwards not part of Indian mainstream? If they are, how can their Hindu counterpart then be part of mainstream? No one maintains that dalits are not part of Indian mainstream.

Is then main problem their religion? Is Islam then part of the problem? Even if it is so these low caste dalit and backward caste Muslims hardly live 'Islamised' life style. As pointed out above they are quite indistinct from their Hindu counterparts in every way and many of them, like Meo Muslims, follow all 'Hindu' customs and traditions. The Tablighi movement was started in mid-twentieth century to 'Islamise' the Meos but until today Meos could not be 'Islamised' as Tablighi movement desired and they still cling to their own native customs and traditions.

Then there are Nuts of Rajasthan and also Saperas (the snake catchers) in Maharashtra. They are hardly aware of their Islamic identity and their conversion to Islam has hardly brought any change in their culture and way of living. Perhaps nothing changed except their names and in many cases even names did not change. And let us not forget that these Muslims constitute the overwhelming majority of Indian Muslims today. How these Muslims should then be treated? As aliens and away from mainstream? How strange then if they are treated as not part of mainstream?

Now let us discuss the case of urban upper caste Muslims who insist on their Islamic identity. The fact is that even these Muslims should be categorised as Indo-Muslims as far as their cultural identity is concerned. Also, most of these Muslims never attend madrasas. They go to English medium schools or to regional language schools and in North India lower caste among them send their children to Hindi medium schools. Of course there are some Muslims who go to Urdu medium schools.

Now the Sachar Committee Report has established that only 4 per cent Muslim children go to madrasas and that means only a tiny percentage of Muslims sends their children to madrasas. Sending to madrasas is also often mentioned as the reason for being aloof from Indian mainstream. Even that myth has now been exploded by the data provided by Sachar Committee report.

It is also said that since Muslims feel strongly about certain events taking place in Muslim countries like Palestine or Iraq or Mecca and hence they are not truly Indian. Now millions of Hindu Indians are living in U.K., USA and other western countries and have become citizens of those countries. Do they feel strongly about events in India or not? Do they lobby for India in those respective countries on some important issues or not? Should they be then accepted as part of American or British mainstream or not? How would they feel if natives of those countries reject them?

Most of the Arab countries are friendly to India and India until recently has supported the Arab cause (though now since NDA came to power there has been clear re-orientation in foreign policy and almost same orientation continues during the UPA Government which feels itself closer to USA position in the Arab world). Of course there are some Muslims who over-react on these events and a section of Muslim leadership incites them to do so to grind their own political axe. The secular Muslim intellectuals should strive to change this situation and educate the Muslim masses in this respect.

It is also not correct that Muslims are over zealous in religious matters. It is the general characteristics of Indian society. Any anthropologist who has done field studies will bear this out. In fact, and this is very interesting to note, that one anthropological study in West Bengal suggests that all life cycle rituals in Bengal among Hindus as well as Muslims are similar and life cycle rituals mean rituals from birth to death. Things are not very different in other parts of India.

Thus it will be seen that it is sheer myth spread by communal forces that Muslims are not part of mainstream and need to be forced into it. They are as much part of mainstream as any India. Now as Hindu militancy is intensifying Christians are also being seen as separate from mainstream though they are harbingers of modern education in India and run so many prime educational institutions in which even most of the communal leaders have been educated.

Muslims are undoubtedly quite backward as very well brought out by Sachar Committee report and blame does not lie with Muslims for their backwardness except in limited sense. It is more due to neglect of successive governments and it is as much responsibility of Government as that of Muslim leaders to pull them out of this backwardness.

10

Democracy, Parochialism and Peace

The way Raj Thackeray has provoked street violence in Mumbai and the way state government handled it has indeed shamed all those who stand for democracy and peace. It is not for the first time that peace in Mumbai has been broken. Citizens of Mumbai have experienced it time and again. Maharashtra Navnirman Sena is after all offshoot of Shivsena and Bal Thackeray, Raj Thackeray's guru and his ideological inspiration, has done it many number of times.

Shiv Sena is not only a parochial force, it is also communal and takes pride in being supporter of Hindutva. MNS has at least, so far has avoided brush with Hindutva and for the first time has manifested its aggressive parochial face and all the commentators agree that it has been done with a view of election next year. MNS could not make much headway in Mumbai Municipal corporation election and drew almost blank.

The MNS is eager to cut Shiv Sena to size and it can do so only by hijacking its regional chauvinist card, which Raj has done successfully or so it seems. Thousands of north Indians got panicky and many of them left for their homes in U.P. and Bihar. The state Government deliberately avoided taking action and when it arrested Raj it was for few hours and he easily got bail.

It is said that the state government deliberately delayed action to cut into Shiv Sena vote bank. If Shiv Sena remains strong the Congress-NCP government is threatened. Thus by weakening Shivsena by letting Raj Thackeray's MNS prey on Shivsena Vote bank, the Congress-NCP Government can feel secure. The BJP has also reacted strongly and blamed the state government for delaying action to promote its own interests. The BJP's anger is understandable as it is an ally of Shiv Sena in Maharashtra and any threat to Shiv Sena is threat to itself.

Mr. L.K. Advani, opposition's candidate for Prime Ministerial post, denounced Raj Thackeray's regional chauvinism as divisive. What a charge! Mr. Advani plays no less divisive politics. Raj is playing divisive politics between Maharashtrians and North Indians and Advani is apt at dividing Hindus and Muslims. All three i.e. BJP, Shiv Sena and MNS are playing narrow provincial or religious chauvinism.

In fact this is main weakness of Indian democracy today. Indian politics has been reduced to mere identity politics, be it caste, religious or regional identities. May be our constitution is ideal but our practicing politicians are not. They revel in exploiting narrow sentiments. The ideals of the Constitution are part of political rhetoric or at best constitution can be invoked only in the courts, particularly the Supreme Court.

The Criminal procedure Code, though drafted by the British more than hundred and fifty years ago, too, is an ideal document for maintaining law and order in the country. Like the Constitution it too, remains on paper as far as powerful politicians are concerned. Had Criminal procedure code been sincerely applied much of our communal, caste and other parochial problems could have been solved. It is now quite usual for politicians to play these parochial sentiments to target easy votes on emotional grounds.

IPC section 153 A & B had been sincerely applied to all those who use narrow parochial; ideology, neither there would have been 33000 communal riots in post-independence India nor peace would have been so often disturbed in our country. But problem is one cannot prosecute any politician or government servant without prior permission of state government and state government would never grant permission without weighing its political implications.

One can cite numerous examples. If the Narsimha Rao Government had taken action against BJP leaders like L.K.Advani, Uma Bharti, Sadhvi Rithambara and several others under section 153 A of Criminal Procedure Code, neither Babri Masjid would have been demolished nor post-Babri demolition riots in Mumbai, Surat, Ahmedabad, Bhopal, Kanpur, Kolkatta and several other places would have taken place thus sparing shame to our country and our secular values.

It is well known that Uma Bharti and Sadhvi Rithambara were using extremely foul language to provoke Hindu sentiments against Muslims and it was repeatedly pointed out to Mr. Narsimha Rao but he never allowed concerned authorities to take action. What happened as a result of such deliberate inaction is now history. The story of Gujarat 2002 is no different. But there state government itself was directly involved in provoking communal violence so who would invoke action against the culprits.

It would be in order to mention here that when Justice Suresh of Bombay High Court disqualified a Shiv Sena candidate on grounds of using religion to appeal to voters in Vile Parle constituency in 1995 election and also disqualified Bal Thackeray himself from voting for five years for making provocative speeches it has considerable effect on Shiv Sena rhetoric. It was from that time onwards that Bal Thackeray became somewhat cautious in mounting direct attacks on minorities.

Also, the election commission for decades ignored provocative speeches including Ramjanambhoomi rhetoric by BJP leaders and it helped aggravate the situation and two general elections were fought by BJP on communal rhetoric without any action by election commission. It was after Seshan, the then Chief Election Commissioner, began to take action that some restraint was observed by politicians in freely using communal rhetoric, if right from beginning action had been taken by election commissions from first general election in 1951 our elections would have been free of religious parochialism and our secular democracy would have been more rich in content.

The Maharashtra Government too deliberately avoided taking action in time against Raj Thackeray's regional chauvinistic rhetoric that several north Indians were attacked and one Maharashtrian lost his life in Nashik. As pointed out the delay was deliberate to draw political advantage.

Politics is essential part of democracy but unfortunately our politics is all about power by any means fair or foul. Secular democracy can have meaning only if our politics is based on values, not on considerations of wining elections. Elections should be oriented towards issues, not to religious, caste or regional chauvinism. Unfortunately no elections so far has been fought on issues. All elections have been fought on emotional issues though one cannot say people's problems were never raised. I am referring to general thrust.

There seems to be only one exception: post-emergency elections. Emergency was an overwhelming event and people were very angry against Mrs. Gandhi and Sanjay Gandhi who had acted as extra-constitutional authority. The then Jansangh had also merged with Janta Party which defeated the Indira Gandhi-led Congress and had taken vow at Mahatma Gandhi's Samadhi for Gandhian socialism and secularism and thus no party was left to exploit parochial issues.

Some drastic measures are needed to re-orient our elections towards secular values and people's problems rather than people's parochial identities. There is one dilemma, however. Those castes and communities, who have been left out and have been deprived of their just share in fruits of development or share in power, are bound to invoke their primordial identities to demand justice.

Such a dilemma can be resolved only by adhering to principles of justice to make democracy all-inclusive for all sections of society. One can also argue that Raj is trying to invoke Maharashtrian identity for justice to Maharashtrian's being left out from fruits of development. Even if it is so it cannot be resolved through street violence. No democracy would admit of it.

It should be resolved through political processes and particularly through constructive dialogue keeping common people's safety and security. Raj was definitely responsible for provoking street violence. It cannot be acceptable in any case. It would be wrong to say that gross injustice is being done to Maharashtrians in Maharashtra. North Indians do not hold plum jobs either in private sector or in public sector. Quite to the contrary; they all are self-employed being petty hawkers or milk vendors or workers in various private small-scale industries.

As for straining Bombay's infra-structure all statistical data shows that more Maharashtrians are migrating from various parts of Maharashtra than people from North India. All those who come to Mumbai contribute to its growth in their own way. Life in Mumbai will be severely affected if these North Indians are expelled or stop coming to Mumbai. And in this way people's right to move freely in the country will also be under attack.

One can reduce effect of caste, communal and regional emotions by making elections all inclusive, like democracy should be. Today the British system of first past the pole system of winning elections has encouraged such parochial electioneering. If this system is changed in favor of 51% votes of the votes caste electoral appeal will have to be more inclusive and less parochial. Will opticians agree? That will save our secular democracy.

11

Identity and Social Exclusion-Inclusion – a Muslim Perspective

In multi-religious, multi-cultural democracies problem of identity and social exclusion-inclusion become extremely important. Under authoritarian societies due to suppression problem of exclusion remains hidden and does not surface until it is gravely aggravated. But a democratic society, being open and based on rights, question of identity and social exclusion and inclusion becomes very important and even determines its very dynamics. A vibrant democratic society always remains sensitive to the question of exclusion of any section of society.

For social exclusion several factors play their role. A caste hierarchy can account for neglect of those at the bottom; a class society may ignore those who belong to lower classes. A multi-religious society may work against those belonging to religious minorities and multi-ethnic or multi-cultural societies may marginalize ethnicities which do not constitute core culture or ethnicity.

In economically backward and under-developed countries the problem of exclusion becomes much more acute in view of scarce resources. Even in advanced economies like those of Western countries exclusion both on the basis of race and class is a well-known phenomenon. The African Americans in America are victims of racial prejudice even today and incidence of poverty among them continues to be very high. America is not only a highly developed country but also economically most advanced. It has highly developed democratic institutions. And yet it cannot claim total inclusion of all sections of society. White majority monopolizes major chunk of all resources.

The western countries were mono-religious and mono-cultural for centuries. The very concept of pluralism and multi-culturalism was unknown among them. The term multi-culturalism was coined by western social scientist only in post-colonial era when large number of workers from ex-colonies began to migrate to metropolitan countries. The western countries like U.K., France, Germany, Sweden, Holland etc. became multi-cultural as migrants were from African and Asian countries.

Another term coined was pluralism, which signified multi-religious and multi-cultural nature of these post-colonial western countries. Post-Second World War there was great demand for workers in these European countries to meet requirement for human resources as due to war large number of Europeans were killed resulting in shortage of human power and reconstruction of economies needed more and more human power. However, later on children of these migrant workers were borne and educated in these metropolitan countries and became their natural citizens with awareness of their rights and privileges.

They began to demand equal rights and equal job opportunities, though not equal share in power as they were mostly tiny minorities. This resulted in racial tension, particularly in U.K., France and Germany. These countries continue to experience these racial and cultural conflicts and the question of exclusion and inclusion has become very important. In France there was revolt by some youth last year and the violence, including burning cars and stoning police went on for several weeks and police found it very challenging to control it.

The sociologists pointed out that the reason for this violence by the youth was their marginalization, high rates of unemployment among them or generally getting low paid jobs which other French people refuse to take up. These young African Muslims were mostly borne in France though their parents had migrated from Algeria, Morocco etc. The Government had to announce series of measures to contain this conflict. Though these measures were far from satisfactory yet these measures gave them some sense of inclusion and the violence abated.

The bombings on 7/7 on London underground was also explained by many scholars in the light of marginalization of these young Pakistanis in U.K., though that was not the only reason. Brainwashing such marginalized youth becomes much easier. They are made to see the White majority as the 'enemy' and unacceptable other. They also become enemy in faith and killing them is justified. Thus there are very complex factors involved in terrorism and terrorist acts.

Whenever such acts of terrorism take place the western leaders (Bush and Blair included) give statements 'our vales, our freedom, our democracy' is at stake and President Bush said, after 9/11 why they (the terrorists) 'hate us, hate our freedom and democracy'. After 7/7 Blair also spoke similar language. The obvious assumption is we westerners have universal values like freedom and democracies and these Afro-

Asians hold authoritarianism dear to themselves and reject concepts of freedom and democracy.

Thus though western social scientists did coin terms like multi-culturalism and religious pluralism, the westerners as a whole, have hardly imbibed these concepts or even while accepting them mentally, these concepts have not touched their hearts and souls. Thus in western societies the problem of exclusion of primordial-identity based minorities is very deep rooted and will not go away easily.

Many Indians have richly contributed to economies and services in U.K., USA and Canada, yet they are victims of social prejudices. They are still far away from being fully integrated in social, cultural and economic sense. They are full citizens of these western countries yet they experience social and cultural exclusion. Racial prejudices still continue to be powerful barriers to full integration in western societies.

Thus it will be seen that social exclusion is playing important role universally. In most of the countries religious and cultural minorities are experiencing social exclusion. One can say social exclusion is to some extent natural (though it should not be) as cultural and religious minorities are migrants from outside and these migrations are just half a century old. These migrations had begun just after 2nd World War. It will take long time for these minorities to become completely naturalized.

In case of India and other Asian countries it is not so. The Asian countries in general and India in particular has always been multi-cultural, multi-religious and multi-ethnic. India has been bewilderingly diverse in this sense for thousands of years. Be they Buddhists, Jains, Christians or Muslims, they have existed in this country and have not, unlike western countries, migrated from outside.

Some Muslims who came as invaders from outside centuries ago, or accompanies these invaders from Central or Western Asia have long become integral part of this country and totally forgotten their foreign identity. No Muslim in India has any awareness of his foreign origin nor he tries to trace his ancestry to outsiders, be they Syeds, Sheikhs or Pathans. And those who came from outside centuries ago are a small minority and an overwhelming majority is of Muslims who converted from Indian stock and belong to lower castes.

The Christians too are not of foreign origin and they are also mostly converts either from low caste Hindus or tribals. The Christians of foreign origin never settled down in India. They kept their distance from Christians of local origin. The Buddhists, Jains and Sikhs are, of course, all Indian origin. Yet the question of exclusion remains important for all minorities but much more so for Christians and Muslims. Christians are a small minority whereas Muslims are a very large minority and hence their exclusion from social, cultural, economic and political processes poses much greater problems.

Democratic processes create greater awareness among people and greater the awareness, greater will become nature of the problem. Also after independence modern secular education has spread much faster than before and though percentage of education among Muslims is lower than average, yet it has increased considerably. Education certainly increases awareness and increased awareness about social, economic or political exclusion creates greater challenges for political management.

Socio-political Exclusion Main Cause of Partition

Our country saw the tragedy of partition at the time of independence. This partition was also direct result of sense of socio-political exclusion and fear of further exclusion in united independent India on the part of Muslim educated elite. The British colonial rule provided opportunities for more education, particularly to the scions of jagirdars ;(feudal lords) and it was this educated Muslim elite which headed partition movement.

It is interesting to note that Muslim Ulama who had their roots among poor and illiterate masses never provided any leadership to the partition movement. On the contrary, they vehemently opposed it. The Jami'at-ul-Ulama-i-Hind (JUH) remained staunch ally of the Indian National Congress and even accepted leadership of Mahatma Gandhi and opposed the two-nation theory of Jinnah. Maulana Husain Ahmed Madani, then chief of JUH wrote a book *Muttahida Qaumiyyat aur Islam* (Composite Nationalism and Islam) and exposed the fallacies of two nation theory.

Thus partition was direct result of sense of exclusion from economic and political share in power among the educated elite and Jinnah, a western educated Muslim and a trained lawyer from England, rather than any religious leader provided both theoretical and political leadership to the Pakistan movement. The Ulama, on the other hand, led by Maulana Abul Kalam Azad and Maulana Husain Ahmad Madani, opposed partition vehemently putting full faith in the programme of Indian National Congress and its secular philosophy.

No doubt, the Constitution of India promulgated on 26th January 1950 fulfilled the promise the Congress leaders made to minorities. The constitutional philosophy is all inclusive. Even Scheduled Castes and Tribes were given reservations. But the Constitutional spirit was never translated into practice. In practice there was not only non-fulfillment of constitutional promise but downright neglect of minorities, especially the Muslims.

The Christians and Muslims, and particularly the Muslims suffer from double disadvantage: they are converts from low caste Hindus and traditionally low caste Hindus suffered from total exclusion and Christians and Muslims also became victims of religious prejudices, thanks to communal propaganda. Thus Christians and Muslims have been doubly excluded from socio-economic and political processes.

For forty years the Congress wielded power at the Centre and also in many states but despite its pro-minority sympathy and commitment to secularism, Muslims were subjected to deliberate neglect. Undoubtedly the Congress propounded secular ideology but it could not even provide even security of life and property to Muslims, let alone ensure their due participation in economic development and educational achievements.

A series of communal riots started from Jabalpur in 1961 onwards and decade of eighties was full of communal violence from Moradabad in 1980 to Mumbai riots of 1992-93. In between many major riots took place in Biharsharif, Meerut, Baroda, Neli (Assam), Bhivandi-Mumbai, Ahmedabad, Meerut (in 1987 again), Bhagalpore and 300 riots when Mr. L.K.Advani took out Rathyatra (which Times of India described as bloodyatra). Thus whole decade of 1980s was a bloody decade and Muslims began to feel terribly insecure.

In post-partition riots more than 35,000 lives were lost and properties worth hundreds of crores destroyed. The Congress swore by secularism but could not effectively provide protection to Muslims from communal violence. Let alone inclusion of Muslims in economic development, the government could not even provide security of life to them.

Also, communal forces of Sangh Parivar continued to question loyalty of Muslims on one hand, and, accused the Congress 'appeasement of Muslims', on the other. This was most ridiculous of all communal propaganda. The Muslim minority was continually falling behind both in economic and educational field and yet the BJP launched an aggressive propaganda offensive of appeasement of Muslims. Nothing could be more absurd.

That Muslims were very backward, falling behind Dalits, who at least benefited to some extent from reservation policy, Muslims could not even avail of reservation. They did avail of reservation in educational institution in some southern states like Tamil Nadu, Kerala and Karnataka and that is why educational status of Muslims in these states is far better than that of Muslims in north.

The Muslims, generally being converts from low caste Hindus continued to follow those caste-based professions like weavers (large number of Muslims in India are weavers), dyers, bangle-makers, Malis, Faqirs, lalbegis, grave diggers, carders dhobis and so on. They are naturally mostly self-employed. These artisans and manual workers are facing acute crisis due to liberalization and globalization also.

The Gopal Singh High Commission report in early eighties and Sachar Committee report in 2006 have provided wealth of data[1] on economic and educational data on Indian Muslims to show backwardness of Muslims in socio-economic status. Both these reports bring out vividly exclusion of Muslims in these fields. In political field too Muslims never got representations in proportions to their population. The number of M.P.s did not even reach 10 per cent in any elected Parliament[2]. It is even worse when it comes to state assemblies. In BJP ruled state of M.P. there is a single MLA though there is Muslim population of 7 per cent in M.P. This speaks volumes about exclusion of Muslims even from political power.

The Gopal Singh High Power commission report was put in cold storage and was not even tabled in Parliament. When Shri V.P.Singh became Prime Minister and convened a meeting of Muslim leaders and intellectuals, I asked him about implementation of Gopal Singh High Powered Commission report. He, to my shock, was not even aware of any such report. He promised to table it in Parliament and he seemed to be sincere about it but his government fell before he could table it. And it was quietly forgotten during the period of Narsimha Rao. It was never tabled. And one could not expect it to be tabled during the BJP led government.

When the UPA government came to power it promised to take concrete steps for welfare of minorities and Sachar Committee was appointed. The Committee has done its work painstakingly and submitted its report but big question is whether this time it would be implemented.

The Muslim leadership at various levels is holding seminars, meetings and demonstration for implementation of Sachar Committee report. Prime Minster Shri Manmohan Singh has also given assurance for its implementation. But no concrete steps have been announced so far. May be these steps will be announced nearer 2009 elections as a political soap.

It is because of this exclusion of certain castes and communities that identity becomes such an important player in democratic politics. Among religious communities there is question of exclusion of Christians and Muslims, more so Muslims, among caste communities there is exclusion of Dalits and backwards and among regional communities there is exclusion of certain regions like North-East etc.

The excluded communities mobilize their respective identities for putting pressure on the system. Immediately after independence many people felt that we should emphasize only one identity and that is national identity, all other identities should be de-emphasized, if not forgotten. But it was mere idealistic talk. As long as there is exclusion of some, identities will come into play.

Both Muslim and Dalit identities played very powerful role in pre-independence days. Jinnah mobilizing Muslim and Ambedkar Dalit identities. While Ambedkar could win reservations by way of Poona pact in 1935 there was no such luck for Muslim separatist movement and our country fell apart before independence.

Thus in a democratic society identities can play constructive and creative as well destructive role. If corrective steps are not taken in time to do away with exclusion, identity mobilization is the only alternative left. Injustices leading to exclusion can be fought only by appeal to the concerned identity. One cannot talk of only national identity unless national policies are inclusive of all sections of society contained in the nation. Thus in today's India we cannot expect Nation. Those who monopolize all resources can talk of national identity but those left out cannot.

In political field even upper castes are mobilizing people of their caste on the basis of caste identity. Identity has become a potential weapon in the hands of politicians today. Whole politics in first past the poll parliamentary system is based unabashedly on caste and communal identities without even any honorable exception. Mayavati in U.P. came to power by first invoking Dalit identity and raising abusive slogans like *tilak tarazu talwar* (i.e. Brahmins, Banya and Rajput) *inko maro jute char* and then subsequently by raising placating slogan for these upper caste (*hathi nahin ganesh hai*).

Ideally speaking the question of exclusion should not have arisen but thanks to it these identities are playing powerful role in our political system. Not only that reservations for jobs for excluded sections cannot be done away with, more and more categories will have to be included and even there is talk of including private sector in reservation of jobs. It may not be possible immediately but either the private sector will have to come forward voluntarily with some scheme to include these low castes and tribes in offering jobs or government may have to take steps.

Of course Muslims have no chance to be included in reservation but some sections of Muslims constituting most backward castes among them or Dalits among them (about 4 per cent according to Sachar Committee) may have to be offered reservation. The Sachar Committee has recommended this measure.

All parties are based on vote banks of their own or coalition of certain castes and communities. This is very essential in a way for correcting historical injustices as far as low caste and backward religious communities are concerned. Muslims are now being wooed by several caste and regional parties. Both RJD in Bihar and SP and BSP in U.P. have tried to attract Muslims along with OBCs and Dalits. Still Muslims have not got much out of it as far as economic inclusion is concerned but have at least earned security of life and property to some extent.

Thus it will be seen that exclusion and inclusion in our complexly diverse society will continue to play important role in political dynamics of our country. Total exclusion of any caste or community can prove disastrous for our democratic polity. Political wisdom demands that our politicians should take steps for gradual inclusion of all backward sections of our society. Even incremental inclusion will greatly help in stabilizing our polity.

INDEX

Educational Backwardness

Table 1

Graduates as proportion of population by the Age-Groups All India 2004-2005.

Age Groups	*Hindus*			*Muslims*	*Other Minorities*
	Gen	*OBC'S*	*SCS/STS*		
20-30 years	18.6	6.5	3.3	4.5	11.6
30-40 years	16.8	4.6	2.3	3.3	9.2
40-50 years	14.6	3.2	1.5	2.8	8.1
51 years and above	9.8	1.9	0.9	2.1	5.7
Total	15.3	4.4	2.2	3.4	8.9

Source:-Estimated from NSSO (2004-2005)61st, Round, SCH, 10. Social, Economic and educational status of the Muslim community of India-A report prepared by Justice Rajinder Sachar committee appointed by the Prime Minister's High level committee, chapter no 4,pp. 67.

Table 2

Literates as proportion of population by Age-Groups 2004-2005

Age Groups	*Hindus*			*Muslims*	*Others*
	Gen	*OBC*	*SC/ST'S*		
6-13 years	90.2	80.8	74.7	74.6	88.5
14-15 years	95.7	87.5	80.0	79.5	91.9
16-17 years	95.0	85.2	78.6	75.5	91.3

(Contd.)

(Contd.Table 2)

Age Groups	*Hindus*			*Muslims*	*Others*
	Gen	*OBC*	*SC/ST'S*		
18-22 years	91.4	76.9	65.0	70.5	85.8
23 years and above	74.0	50.6	36.5	46.1	67.0
Total	80.5	63.4	52.7	59.9	75.2

Source: - Estimated from NSSO (2004-2005)61st, Round, SCH, 10. Social, Economic and educational status of the Muslim community of India-A report prepared by Justice Rajinder Sachar committee appointed by the Prime Minister's High level committee, chapter no 4 pp. 54.

Table 3
Children currently studying as a proportion of population by Age-Groups 2004-2005

Age Groups	*Hindus*			*Muslims*	*Other Minorities*
	Gen	*OBC*	*SC/STS*		
6-13 years	19.1 (17.3)	36.1 (35.5)	25.7 (27.4)	14.0 (15.1)	5.1 (4.8)
14-15 years	24.3 (19.9)	36.1 (35.2)	21.4 (25.2)	12.2 (14.5)	6.0 (5.3)
16-17 years	28.9 (21.1)	33.7 (35.0)	20.2 (24.7)	10.7 (14.0)	6.3 (5.1)
18-22 years	34.0 (20.8)	30.5 (34.4)	17.7 (25.5)	10.2 (13.9)	7.6 (5.5)
23 years and above	35.6 (23.9)	29.2 (35.1)	18.3 (24.1)	7.4 (10.9)	9.5 (5.9)

Source: - Estimated from NSSO (2004-2005)61st, Round, SCH, 10. Social, Economic and educational status of the Muslim community of India-A report prepared by Justice Rajinder Sachar committee appointed by the Prime Minister's High level committee, Chapter No 4, pp. 72.

Economy and Employment

Table 1
Worker Population Ratios (WPR) by Socio-Religious categories 2004-2005 (Principal and Subsidiary Status, 15-64 years)

Social Group		*Urban*	*Rural*	*Male*	*Female*	*Total*
Hindus	All Hindus	53.1	70.3	84.9	46.1	65.8
	SCS/STS	56.3	74.5	87.3	54.9	71.4
	OBC'S	56.4	70.5	85.8	48.3	67.3
	UC	49	63.5	80.8	33.1	57.4
Muslims		51.1	57	84.6	25.2	54.9
Other minorities		51.6	70.2	81.8	47.2	64.5
All		52.7	68.9	84.6	43.6	64.4

Source:- Social, Economic and educational status of the Muslim community of India-A report prepared by Justice Rajinder Sachar committee appointed by the Prime Minister's High level committee, Chapter No 5, pp. 110.

Table No:-2
Unemployment rate by Social Religious categories, all age groups daily status

	Hindus				*Mus-lims*	*Other mino-rities*	*All*
	All Hindus	*SCS/STS*	*OBC'S*	*UC*			
Urban	8.1	10.5	8.2	6.8	8.1	10.9	8.3
Rural	8.0	10.0	7.4	6.0	8.4	10.8	8.2
Male	7.2	10.2	7.0	5.1	8.1	10.2	7.8
Female	9.0	9.9	8.8	8.0	9.2	12.2	9.2

Source:- Social, Economic and educational status of the Muslim community of India-A report prepared by Justice Rajinder Sachar committee appointed by the Prime Minister's High level committee, Chapter No 5, pp. 110

Table 3

Distribution of workers in each Socio-Religious categories by Enterprise-Type in rural and urban areas, 2004-2005 all workers aged 15-64 years.

	Hindus				*Muslims*	*Other minorities*	*All*
	All Hindus	*SCS/ STS*	*OBC'S*	*UC*			
			Urban				
Informal sector	76.9	78.5	82.2	71.4	92.1	76.4	79.1
Proprietary male	59.2	58.6	65.7	53.6	76.2	55.4	61.5
Proprietary female	5.7	6.3	5.9	5.2	7.4	5.5	5.9
Partnership with members of the same household	2.8	2.4	2.5	3.4	2.8	4.0	2.9
Partnership with members of the other household	2.3	1.5	2.3	2.6	1.4	2.8	2.2
Others	6.9	9.8	5.8	6.5	4.3	8.6	6.6
Formal sector	23.1	21.5	17.8	28.6	7.9	23.6	20.9
Govt/pub sector	15.4	16.6	11.3	18.4	5.6	15.5	13.9
Pub/pvt sector	7.7	4.9	6.5	10.2	2.3	8.1	6.9
Total	100	100	100	100	100	100	100

(Contd.)

(Contd.Table 3)

	Hindus				*Muslims*	*Other minorities*	*All*
	All Hindus	*SCS / STS*	*OBC'S*	*UC*			
			Urban				
			Rural				
Informal sector	87.7	88.1	89.8	82.8	94.2	88.1	88.5
Proprietary male	67.7	67.6	70.6	61.9	72.6	53.0	67.3
Proprietary female	11.8	11.2	11.9	12.6	13.7	23.5	12.9
Partnership with members of the same household	1.7	1.5	1.7	1.9	1.6	4.9	1.9
Partnership with members of the other household	1.3	1.0	1.3	1.5	1.0	0.8	1.2
Others	5.2	6.7	4.3	4.9	5.2	5.8	5.2
Formal sector	12.3	11.9	10.2	17.2	5.8	11.9	11.5
Govt/ public sector	9.0	8.8	7.2	13.0	4.8	9.7	8.5
Pub/pvt ltd company	3.3	3.1	3.0	4.2	1.0	2.2	3.0
Total	100	100	100	100	100	100	100

Source:- Social, Economic and educational status of the Muslim community of India-A report prepared by Justice Rajinder Sachar committee appointed by the Prime Minister's High level committee, Chapter No 5, pp. 113.

Table 4

Distribution of workers in each socio-religious categories by enterprise –Type for male and female workers 2004-2005 (All workers aged 15-64 years)

	Hindus				*Muslims*	*Other minorities*	*All*
	All Hindus	*SCS/STS*	*OBC'S*	*UC*			
			Male				
Informal sector	81.0	83.1	85.1	74.0	92.6	80.4	82.7
Proprietary male	71.1	72.6	76.2	63.3	84.2	68	72.8
Proprietary female	0.6	0.6	0.6	0.5	0.4	0.6	0.6
Partnership with members of the same household	2.3	1.9	2.1	3.1	2.3	3.7	2.4
Partnership with members of the other household	2.0	1.3	2.1	2.5	1.4	2.1	1.9

(Contd.)

(Contd.Table 4)

	Hindus				*Muslims*	*Other minorities*	*All*
	All Hindus	*SCS/STS*	*OBC'S*	*UC*			
			Male				
Formal sector	19.0	16.9	14.9	26.0	7.4	19.6	17.3
Govt/pub sector	12.9	12.8	9.9	16.9	5.6	13.6	11.9
Pub/pvt sector	6.1	4.1	5.0	9.1	1.8	6.1	5.4
Total	100	100	100	100	100	100	100
			Female				
Informal sector	88.3	89.4	91.1	82.3	95.3	87.9	89
Proprietary male	44.8	44.3	49.8	37.1	38.4	30.4	42.8
Proprietary female	32.2	32.1	32.0	32.8	47.7	42	34.8

(Contd.)

(Contd.Table 4)

	Hindus				*Muslims*	*Other minorities*	*All*
	All Hindus	*SCS/STS*	*OBC'S*	*UC*			
			Male				
Partnership with members of the same household	1.8	1.6	1.8	1.9	1.8	5.9	2.2
Partnership with members of the other household	0.9	0.3	0.9	1.0	0.4	0.9	0.8
Others	8.6	10.5	6.8	9.6	7.0	8.8	8.4
Formal sector	11.7	10.6	8.9	17.7	4.7	12.1	11.0
Govt/ public sector	8.7	7.8	6.0	14	3.5	9.8	8.2
Pub/pvt ltd company	3.1	2.7	2.9	3.7	1.2	2.3	2.8
Total	100	100	100	100	100	100	100

Source:- Social, Economic and educational status of the Muslim community of India-A report prepared by Justice Rajinder Sachar committee appointed by the Prime Minister's High level committee, Chapter No 5, pp.114.

Table 5

Percentage of regular salaried/wage non-agricultural workers in each SRC employed in Govt/ Public and large Private sectors

SRCS	*All*	*Male*	*Female*	*Urban*	*Rural*
	Govt. /Pub. /Pvt. / Ltd.	*Govt. /Pub. /Pvt. / Ltd.*	*Govt. /Pub. /Pvt. / Ltd.*	*Govt. /Pub. /P vt. / Ltd.*	*Govt. /Pub. / Pvt. / Ltd.*
All	34.2/13.1	34/13.8	35.1/10.2	31.5/14.6	39.2/10.5
All Hindus	35.3/13.9	35.3/14.6	35.2/10.7	32.8/15.3	39.5/11.4
SCS/STS	39.4/9.5	41.3/9.4	32.4/9.9	36.7/8.7	42.9/10.5
OBC'S	30.4/12.8	30.4/13.1	30.0/11.4	27.3/14.0	34.6/11.1
UC	37.4/17.1	36.4/18.6	41.7/10.6	35.2/18.8	43.2/12.5
MUSLIMS	23.7/6.5	23.0/6.5	29.4/6.8	19.4/7.4	33.3/4.8
OTHER MINORITIES	35.8/12.8	35.1/14.8	37.6/8.0	32.0/16.5	41.8/7.1

Source:- Social, Economic and educational status of the Muslim community of India-A report prepared by Justice Rajinder Sachar committee appointed by the Prime Minister's High level committee, Appendix Chapter No 5, pp. 320.

Government Employment services

Table 1
Muslim Employees in Government sector employment

Depts / Institutions reporting	*Reported number of employees*	*Reported number of Muslim employees*	*Muslims as % to reported employees*
State level departments	4452851	278385	6.3
Railways	1418747	64066	4.5
Banks and RBI	680833	15030	2.2
Security Agencies	1879134	60517	3.2
Postal Service	275841	13759	5.0
Universities	137263	6416	4.7
All Reported	8844669	438173	4.9
Govt Employment			
Central PSUS	687512	22387	3.3
State PSUS	745271	80661	10.8
All PSUS	1432783	103048	7.2

Source:- Social, Economic and educational status of the Muslim community of India-A report prepared by Justice Rajinder Sachar committee appointed by the Prime Minister's High level committee, Appendix Chapter 5, p. 165.

Table 2
Share of Muslims in All India Civil Services 2006

Service	*All officers*	*No. of Muslim officers*	*Muslims as % to all*	*Unconfirmed names*
Civil Service Officers (IAS, IFS, IPS)	8827	285	3.2	10
Direct recruitment through competitive examination	6460	155	2.4	4

(Contd.)

(Contd. Table 2)

Service	*All officers*	*No. of Muslim officers*	*Muslims as % to all*	*Unconfirmed names*
Promoted from State Service	2367	130	5.5	6
Indian Administrative Service	4790	142	3.0	4
Direct recruitment through competitive examination	3542	80	2.3	0
Promoted from state service	1248	62	5.0	4
Indian Foreign Service	828	15	1.8	0
Direct Recruitment	621	12	1.9	0
Grade of IFS (B) Personnel	207	3	1.4	0
Indian Police Service	3209	128	4.0	6
Direct recruitment through competitive examination	2297	63	2.7	4
Promoted from State Service	912	65	7.1	2

- *Source*:-IAS Civil List 2006 Ministry of Public grievances and Pensions Government of India (51st edition), Indian Police Service civil lists 2006, Ministry of Home Affairs, Government of India (50th edition), Indian Foreign Service civil lists 2006 Ministry of External affairs (Government of India).
- Social, Economic and educational status of the Muslim community of India-A report prepared by Justice Rajinder Sachar committee appointed by the Prime Minister's High level committee, Appendix Chapter No 9, p. 166.

Table 3

Share of Muslim Employees in selected Central Government Departments and Institutions

Category / Level of Employment	*Total number of employees*	*Civil services*	*Railways / telegraphs*	*Post and services*	*Security agencies*	*banks*	*Universities*	*PSUS*
Group A	231619	4.8 (35.8)	2.5 (18.7)	3.8 (28.4)	3.1 (23.1)	1.7 (12.7)	3.7 (27.6)	2.3 (17.2)
Group B	122551		3.4 (25.4)	4.4 (32.8)	3.9 (29.1)			2.8 (20.9)
Group C	1486637		4.9 (36.6)	4.8 (35.8)	4.6 (34.3)	2.5 (18.7)	5.4 (40.3)	3.9 (29.1)
Group D	659113		5.0 (37.3)	5.3 (39.6)	4.3 (32.1)			

Source:- Social, Economic and educational status of the Muslim community of India-A report prepared by Justice Rajinder Sachar committee appointed by the Prime Minister's High level committee, Appendix Chapter 9, p. 168.

Table 4

Share of Employment in Indian Railways according to SRC'S (Total Number of Employees 14, 18,747)

Category	*All*	*Hindus*				
		All Hindus	*SCS/ STS*	*Other Hindus*	*Muslims*	*Other Minorities*
Higher positions	1.3	92.8	18.2	74.6	3.0 (22.4)	4.3
Lower Positions	98.7	88.6	22.5	66.1	5.0 (37.3)	6.4
Group 'A'	0.7	93.8	17.8	76.0	2.5 (18.7)	3.7
Group 'B'	0.6	91.5	19.0	72.6	3.4 (25.4)	5.0
Group 'C'	59.7	88.5	22.0	66.5	4.9 (36.6)	6.5
Group 'D'	37.4	88.7	23.4	65.3	5.0 (37.3)	6.3

Source:- Social, Economic and educational status of the Muslim community of India-A report prepared by Justice Rajinder Sachar committee appointed by the Prime Minister's High level committee, Appendix Chapter No 9, pp. 369.

Table 5

Share of employment in National Security Agencies (Total Number of Employees 5, 19, 008)

Category	*All*	*Hindus*		*Other Hindus*	*Muslims*	*Other Minorities*
		All Hindus	*SCS/STS*			
Higher Positions	3.9	87.5	11.7	75.8	3.6 (26.9)	8.9
Lower Positions	96.1	88.7	24.4	64.4	4.6 (34.3)	6.7

(Contd.)

(Contd. Table 5)

Category	*All*	*Hindus*		*Other Hindus*	*Muslims*	*Other Minorities*
		All Hindus	*SCS/STS*			
Group 'A'	1.3	86.0	11.9	74.1	3.1 (23.1)	10.9
Group 'B'	2.6	88.2	11.6	76.6	3.9 (29.1)	7.9
Group 'C'	91.5	88.7	23.8	64.9	4.6 (34.3)	6.7
Group 'D'	4.2	89.3	36.8	52.5	4.3 (32.1)	6.4
Others	0.4	85.3	24.2	61.1	3.3 (24.6)	11.3

Source:- Social, Economic and educational status of the Muslim community of India-A report prepared by Justice Rajinder Sachar committee appointed by the Prime Minister's High level committee, Appendix Chapter 9, pp. 369.

Table 6
Share of Employment in Posts and Telegraphs (Total Number of Employees 275841)

Category	*All*	*Hindus*			*Muslims*	*Other Minorities*
		All Hindus	*SCS/STS*	*Other Hindus*		
Higher Position	1.4	94.8	20.8	3.6	70.5	4.3
Lower Position	98.6	94.2	27.4	10.0	56.9	5.0

(Contd.)

(Contd. Table 6)

Category	*All*	*Hindus*			*Muslims*	*Other Minorities*
		All Hindus	*SCS/STS*	*Other Hindus*		
Group 'A'	0.1	93.7	23.0	3.0	67.7	3.8
Group 'B'	0.3	95.0	20.5	3.6	70.8	4.4
Group 'C'	59.8	94.6	27.6	7.6	59.4	4.8
Group 'D'	38.8	93.6	27.0	13.6	53.1	5.3

Source:- Social, Economic and educational status of the Muslim community of India-A report prepared by Justice Rajinder Sachar committee appointed by the Prime Minister's High level committee, Appendix Chapter No 9, pp. 369.

Data on Communal riots

Table 1
Frequency and Casualties of Communal incidents (1950-2002)

Year	*Incidents*	*Killed*	*Injured*
1950	56	50	256
1954	84	34	512
1955	75	24	457
1956	82	35	575
1957	58	12	316
1958	40	7	369
1959	42	41	1344
1960	26	14	262

(Contd.)

(Contd. Table 1)

Year	*Incidents*	*Killed*	*Injured*
1961	92	108	593
1962	60	43	348
1963	61	26	489
1964	1070	1919	2053
1965	173	34	758
1966	144	45	467
1967	198	301	880
1968	346	133	1309
1969	519	674	2702
1970	521	298	1607
1971	321	103	1330
1972	210	70	1056
1973	242	72	1318
1974	248	87	1123
1975	205	33	890
1976	169	39	794
1977	188	36	1122
1978	230	108	1853
1979	304	261	2379
1980	421	375	2691
1981	319	196	2613
1982	470	238	3025
1983	500	1143	3652
1984	476	445	4836
1985	525	332	3751
1986	768	418	5389
1987	711	383	3860
1988	710	259	3103
1989	922	802	3871
1990	1421	1241	3913
1991	29	877	6370
1992	37	1972	13571

(Contd.)

(Contd. Table 1)

Year	*Incidents*	*Killed*	*Injured*
1993	33	960	4496
1994	8	39	450
1995	17	54	235
1996	20	24	28
1997	70	137	495
1998	600	207	2065
1999	52	43	248
2000	24	91	165
2001	27	56	158
2002	28	1173	2272
Total	13952	14686	68182

Source:-Communal riots after independence A comprehensive Account Asghar Ali Engineer published by Shipra Publications, pp. 223, 224.

References

1. Please see the charts at the end of the article.
2. See chart no.

Table 1

Percentage of Muslim Members in Lok Sabha and Rajya Sabha

Year	*No. of Muslims in Lok Sabha*	*Total No. of M.Ps*	*%*	*Year*	*No. of Muslims in Rajya Sabha*	*Total No. of M.Ps*	*%*
1952	22	499	4.4	1952			
1957	26	499	5.2	1958			
1962	23	496	4.6	1964			
1967	30	520	5.8	1970			
1971/2	30	520	5.8	1976			
1977	32	544	5.9	1982	27	233	11.59
1980	47	531	8.9	1988	22		9.44
1982	46	554	8.5				
1984	42	517	7.8	1994	20		8.33
1989	32	531	6.0	2000	26		10.73
1991	27	533	5.1				
1994	27	544	4.9				
1998	29	545	5.3				
2000	32	545	5.9				

Source: Muslim India 2000.

12

Gujarat Elections and Aftermath

Gujarat has made history. Gujarat is in news ever since genocide of 2002. For every small or big development it remains in news. Gujarat carnage was unparalleled in the history of India and it will continue to be discussed for a long time to come. Like partition of our country it cannot be easily forgotten. Any election in Gujarat will draw into discussion Gujarat carnage. Modi, I maintain, could not have won 2002 election without organizing that carnage nor the 2007 election could he have won without it.

In my opinion it is wrong to maintain that he won election due to economic development he helped achieve in Gujarat. Gujarat is as much polarized today as it was in 2002. Even if Modi had not mentioned anything related to Hindutva, he would have won. Question is only of margin. Now the congress leaders also have admitted it publicly that we had not kept Sonia Gandhi in any illusion about victory in Gujarat. We had told her we cannot win. Only thing is we did not expect him to win with such majority.

He won with such majority for number of reasons one of which was Mayawati's candidates. In many constituencies Dalits voted for Mayawati candidates and in those constituencies congress candidates lost by margin of not more than 5000 votes. Congress would have undoubtedly won in these constituencies had Mayawati not set up her own candidates taking away Dalit votes.

I would also like to throw light on the question as to why Modi continues to appeal Gujarati voters so much that he can win hands down even five years after genocide of 2002? The answer lies in paradigm shift in political ideologies throughout the world. Unfortunately no analyst so far has seen Gujarat election in this perspective.

Up to eighties socialism and socialist ideologies had great appeal for the people. When Indira Gandhi, in late sixties of last century, gave slogan of quit poverty (*Gharibi hatao*) it had electrifying effect on Indian masses; and she instantly emerged as great leader in her own right and all Congress stalwarts like Kamraj, Morarji Desai and Atulya Ghosh and others fell by the roadside. She was voted to power with overwhelming majority.

Similarly in Pakistan when Zulfiqar Ali Bhutto gave slogan of *Roti, Kapda Makan* (bread, cloth and house). He acquired charisma of his own and Ayub fell by the roadside. To this slogan he added, after Bangla Desh war thousand-year war with India and he emerged as an unquestioned leader of Pakistan. However, the basic mantra was *roti, kapda, makan*. Even in Arab countries slogan of socialism brought Jamal Abdan Nasir and Mohammad Ghaddafi to the fore.

But now there is complete paradigm shift in politics. Socialism no longer has any charisma. It has been replaced by religious ideologies or religious fundamentalism throughout the world. Until late eighties Hindutva had no appeal to Indian masses or Islamic ideology to Pakistani people. Today it is politicized religious discourse which has strong appeal.

Also, slogans of basic needs have been replaced by 'development' discourse and development never means fulfilling basic needs like *roti, kapda makan* but development of the rich, increase in the wealth of the haves as today in liberalized economies in the globalised world. For Gujaratis trade and economic prosperity has been their lifeline. Even among Muslims of Gujarat Bohras, Khojas and Memons are rich traders and they will be as much attracted by the development discourse as upper caste Hindu Gujaratis. It is for this reason that Narendra Modi tried to win over Bohras and Khojas by his development discourse. He even had special section for Muslims (Bohras, Khojas etc.) in the economic exhibition arranged by him to showcase his development.

And today in the Hindutva laboratory that Gujarat is combination of economic development and Hindutva ideology is a sure guarantee for political win. And who knows this better than Modi? Modi thus combined development discourse with Hindutva mantra and won elections hands down.

The BJP maintains that Modi was using only development discourse for his campaigning and it was Sonia Gandhi by her remark of '*maut ka saudagar*' that compelled Modi to use Hindutva card and then whole nature of campaign changed. This can hardly convince any reasonable mind. In fact it was planned that Hindutva discourse will be the last minute mantra. Development discourse was thought to be effective but perhaps there was lurking doubt and to dispel that doubt Hindutva discourse had to be use very tactically, throwing entire blame on the opposition after all.

What Mrs. Sonia Gandhi said was in no way contrary to facts. There was enough proof to maintain that Modi had used death and destruction to win 2002 election (which in all probability, he would have lost). In that election there was no reference to any development. 2002 campaign was heavily loaded with Hindutva discourse and he had earned enough bad publicity throughout the world. He could not afford to deploy pure Hindutva discourse in this election.

The Election Commission was also watching and he could not afford to be on the wrong side of law. He, therefore cleverly crafted his winning strategy – to use development and Hindutva at the last stage and hang the blame on Soniaben's 'maut ka saudagar'peg. If he was so sure of 'development factor why did he not use it in 2002 election? On the contrary he is enjoying its after effects even in this election.

There is now another question: will the Gujarat model be as effective in other states? I have my doubts. Even after 2002 win the BJP was saying we will repeat Gujarat model in other states but it lost in several states. The fact is that BJP is in power in M.P. and Rajasthan by itself like in Gujarat and yet these two states have yet to go Gujarat way i.e. they have still not become 'Hindutva laboratory' like Gujarat.

It is an important question: why M.P. and Rajasthan, like Gujarat, could become Hindutva laboratory. Obviously conditions in these two states and caste and community equations are very different. Neither M.P. nor Rajasthan can ever become Hindutva laboratories like Gujarat. Nor development a la Gujarat can be effected in these two states. Obviously Gujarat model cannot be repeated even in these two BJP held states, much less in other states of India.

India is a highly diverse country – bewilderingly diverse, and what is possible in one state cannot happen in other states. Even CPM cannot repeat its model in states other than West Bengal and Kerala otherwise it would have captured other states long ago. Gujarat is more suited for Hindutva as West Bengal and Kerala are more suited for left ideology. In Gujarat similarly is more suited for rightwing Hindutva ideology for number of reasons.

Traders are generally very conservative and are known to be supporters of conservative religion and traditions. For the same reason Gujarat, unlike Maharashtra and other states, never saw any reform movement. The reform movement which brought into existence Swaminarayan sect, itself was very conservative religious reform movement. Today Swaminarayan movement is most popular and hegemonic in Gujarat. Swaminarayan temples are being built wherever these Patel Gujaratis live spending crores of rupees. Huge complexes have come into existence.

Thus Gujarat never experienced modern reform movement like Bengal or Kerala or Maharashtra or Karnataka. And hence the vice-like hold of conservative religion on Gujarat. Narendra Modi has shrewdly exploited this for his political rise. Also by organizing 2002 carnage of Muslims he built his charismatic image and now he is shrewdly combining it with his development discourse.

M.P. and Rajasthan also will face election soon. These states are very different both in economic and political sense. M.P. has already seen change of three chief ministers and the present one carries the stigma of being corrupt as he is facing serious corruption charges. He cannot claim charismatic position as Modi enjoys in Gujarat. Same is the story of Rajasthan. Both in M.P. and Rajasthan still feudal culture is quite strong and modern capitalistic development does not have attraction as Gujarat has.

In Rajasthan VHP tried its best to convert into Gujarat and often held out this threat but it never succeeded. Mrs.

Vasundhara Raje Scindia could hardly employ Hindutva discourse as she comes from a ruling family of Gwalior and has very different experience. Modi, on the other hand, belongs to low Hindu caste of Gujarat and in order to rise to higher status, can employ reactionary religious ideology without any qualms and seek his own revenge for being humiliated all through history.

In U.P. there is no question of BJP using Gujarat model. It has, in Mayawati, met more than its match and she is going strong and has Dalit-Muslim and a section of upper caste votes also. Also, leaders like Rajnathsingh or Kalyan Singh hardly can claim charisma as Modi enjoys. And in present day U.P. it is not possible for BJP to organize Gujarat like genocide to gain any charisma.

Thus it will be seen that Gujarat is what it is on account of its own specificities and BJP's dream of repeating Gujarat can hardly be fulfilled in other states.

13

Knighthood for Salman Rushdie and Muslims

Knighthood conferred on Salman Rushdie by queen of England a few weeks ago has raised a great controversy throughout Islamic world. Some have conferred, in reaction to this title of *Saif Allah* (Allah's Sword) by a group of extremist 'Ulama in Pakistan. The conferment of knighthood on Salman Rushdie has revived the controversy which raged in nineties on his novel *the Satanic Verses.*

Ayatollah Khomeini of Iran who brought about Islamic revolution in Iran in 1979 had issued a fatwa to kill Salman Rushdie for insulting the Prophet of Islam (PBUH). It really became a serious confrontation between Western and Islamic world and it appeared as if the self-fulfilling prediction of 'clash of civilizations' is taking place. The western countries defended Salman Rushdie on grounds of human rights and Islamic World condemned Rushdie for his insolence against the Prophet (PBUH) and his wives.

Salman Rushdie was provided with security by the British government for years at a heavy cost as his life was in danger after Ayatollah Khomeini issued the fatwa. Later on however, though fatwa was not withdrawn it was almost treated as non-existent by authorities in Iran.

Now with conferment of knighthood the controversy has again been revived and angry demonstrations are taking place in many Muslim countries. However, it must be said that these demonstrations are not as extensive and intensive compared to what happened in early nineties. Nevertheless Muslims in general have been offended. It once again raises the question about right of expression and its limits.

Freedom of expression is a sacred right but it does not include right to insult founder of a religion who is held in high esteem by millions of his followers. But west does not agree. It recognizes no such limit. In the west films, novels, plays are written on Christ which go against the Christian beliefs. But Christians in Eastern countries like India do protest against such novels or films. When a film which did not conform to Christian beliefs was shown in India the Christians protested and demanded ban on it. It was allowed to be shown on certain conditions only.

In the West liberalism on one hand, and, indifference towards religion are almost a way of life. No one takes seriously anything written critical of religion or even anti-religion but it is very different in Asiatic countries, particularly in Islamic world in Asia and Africa. Liberalism in these countries is limited to few intellectuals and these intellectuals also often refrain from expressing their views publicly for fear of being ostracized.

Salman Rushdie's book is not even serious critique of Islamic beliefs but ridiculing them. There is difference between attempting a serious critique disagreeing with certain beliefs and very much different to ridicule those beliefs. Rushdie uses technique of magic realism and transforms various characters considered to be sacred by Muslims into radically different forms. For example Jibrail Farishta is transformed into a Bollywood character. One can certainly use these techniques for ordinary characters but not characters like Jibrail through whom, Muslims believe, Prophet (PBUH) received revelation which was compiled in the form of Qur'an. Even Prophet's wives are subjected to this treatment.

This can be hardly acceptable in the cultural and religious ethos in Asia in general and in Islamic world, in particular. Though there is no clash of civilizations but there are significant differences in civilizations and these differences should be respected and accommodated. The limits of freedom of expression are different in degree between western and eastern civilizations.

The latest development in Punjab also throws enough light on this question. It is not only Muslims who get agitated if their religion is ridiculed but also others like Hindus and Sikhs. The controversy between Sikhs and Dera Saccha Sauda assumed huge proportions and Sikhs came out on the streets with swords drawn. The Sikhs felt that the Chief of Dera Saccha Sauda by donning clothes of Guru Gobind Singh has insulted their religion. And even apology from Dera Saccha Sauda does not seem to satisfy them and they are insisting on arresting him and prosecuting him. This is the reality in our countries. The west must appreciate this reality and cannot insist on its own standards of liberalism and individual rights.

Having said this I would like to insist that Salman Rushdie, no doubt has exceeded the tolerance limit of Asians but one should also appreciate his creative talents which cannot go unrecognized. Except his novel *Satanic Verses* his other novels like *Midnight children* and several others are highly appreciated and one has to recognize his talent. It is also true that he is not anti-Muslim. As someone very aptly put it Salman both fights

Muslims and fights for Muslims. It is literally true. He is committed to minority rights and he fights for their rights in U.K. and other countries. We should not judge him by one single novel.

It is also to be noted that it is the right of the U.K. government to confer honor on its citizens. We cannot dictate government of any sovereign country on whom to confer or not to confer honors. No sovereign government will like to be dictated. One can certainly makes ones feelings known through proper channels but should not take to streets and burn flag of that country. Flag represents dignity and sovereignty of a country and insulting someone's flag amounts to insulting that country. It does not befit thinking people to tread over some country's flag or burn it.

It is also important to remember that a creative writer is nothing if not subversive of established values, beliefs and practices. Only thing is that one must be conscious of decent limits of subversion, when it involves religious beliefs. Many beliefs are thought to be religious but are not religious. They pertain more to customs and traditions and social ethos. A writer has to be free to subvert such beliefs or practices.

If one does not have such freedom nothing in the world will change. All great thinkers have been subversive. Even in the Qur'an Prophet Ibrahim (Abraham) (PBUH) has been shown as subversive of beliefs and practices of his people. Prophet Muhammad (PBUH) himself attacked superstitions around idols which Arabs worshipped and showed them the right path.

Thus all prophets have been subversive in one way or the other. Great poets and thinkers like Milton and Iqbal were attracted towards the character of Satan for his; challenging authorities and subverting establishment. His subversiveness makes Satan dynamic and this dynamism makes him attractive to some. But Satanic subversion of course is world apart from prophets' subversion. Satanic subversion is totally negative whereas prophet's subversion is positive in character. Prophetic subversion leads to creation of new world, a world that benefits whole humanity. Satanic subversion, on the other hand, only destroys. Both challenge established authority but prophets challenge authority which is oppressive, exploitative and unjust. Satanic subversion, on the other hand, challenges just authority and leads to darkness and leads to more oppression and exploitation.

Salman Rushdie, in his western environs totally confuses between prophetic and satanic subversions. He is an atheist and does not believe in religion, any religion. And like some other atheists assumes the character of atheistic character and thinks truth is only in his grip and ridicules those who do not agree with him. Thus he ridicules one kind of beliefs to establish another set of atheistic beliefs. And it is in this arrogance of possessing 'truth', he begins to ridicule all those who do not agree with him.

A sober atheist would not disregard truth in others' beliefs. One set of truth should not be set against another set of truth and ridicule it. It is sheer arrogance. A serious atheist like Bertrand Russell attacked certain religious beliefs and practices of the Church only in philosophical sense. Bertrand Russell was himself a great subverter but also believer in the other world based on justice and compassion. He was firmly against war and stood for peace. He courted arrest during First World War opposing Britain's entry into it and shocked whole country. He organized, along with Jean Paul Sartre, trial of war crimes against America committed in Vietnam. He was great peace activist.

Also, if we are true Muslims we should represent best in Islam. Among fundamental values of Islam are wisdom and tolerance. We should make our opposition known in most civilized manner. We should argue with the opponent on the basis of reasoned arguments and never use abusive language. Qur'an warns us not to abuse those who worship other than Allah; they will abuse Allah out of ignorance (6:109).

Thus our protest should be dignified and based on reason. Some politically motivated people exploit religious sentiments by organizing violent street demonstrations, burning effigies and flags. It does not represent best face of Islam and gives an impression Muslims are a fanatic and intolerant lot. It wins more sympathy for Salman Rushdie in the West and defeats the very purpose.

The purpose should not be to demonstrate violently but to convince western people that we are responsible and tolerant people and our religious sensibilities have been hurt. One should go for dialogue not for confrontation. Confrontation takes us nowhere and pays only some power hungry politicians, does not uphold cause of Islam, tolerance and freedom. Freedom of conscience is as central to Islam as to western world. We are, however, failing to communicate this central value of Islam.

14

Terrorism and Educated Youth

In the recent attempted terrorist attacks in Central London and on Glasgow airport, it is alleged, Mr. Kafil Ahmed of Bangalore is involved though his brother Sabil Ahmed is not likely to be directly responsible. While Kafil is aeronautical engineer who has done his M.Phil. in the subject, Sabil Ahmed is a medical doctor. Another doctor also from Bangalore and cousin of Kafil and Sabil Mohammad Hanif was also suspected but he is also not suspected to have played central role. Another persons involved are doctors from Iraq Mr. Bilal Abdulla and from Jordan Mr. Mohammad Asha.

The fact that Kafil, an Indian Muslim, and a highly educated youth is involved has started two controversies – one that Al-Qaeda has reached India and two, that not madrasa product but highly educated youth with technical accomplishment, is involved.

The concept of 'jihad' has come to be inalienably associated with madrasas and it is generally believed that madrasa youth brainwashed in jihadi outlook are involved in acts of terrorism.

This is very erroneous concept. In all major acts of terrorism, whether by Muslims or by others, only modern educated youth is generally involved. Those who plan such attacks are never uneducated or madrasa educated or illiterate poverty ridden youth. No where in the world this has happened.

Who was involved in bombings in 1990s in Aum Sinrikyo of Japan? They were all educated middle class people. The entire ULFA leadership consists of modern educated youth. Same is true of LTTE leadership. The Naxalite movement was also started by University educated people and some of them in the beginning were even had Oxford and Cambridge University degrees.

Marc Sageman in his book *Understanding Terrorist Networks* published in 2004 also concluded that it was not the madrasas that were closely correlated with terrorists or terror, but modern western institutes where students from abroad can end up turning to militant Islam as a way to counter the alienation they experience or the anger they have against the government of the country.

Thus having established that it is highly educated youth who conspire to plan acts of terror it is also necessary to understand why are such educated persons involved? In fact they even make supreme sacrifice of their lives in the process. Firstly, it is only highly educated who understand the policies governments pursue to which they violently react. An illiterate person does not have such understanding and awareness. It is education which brings such awareness to them.

Secondly, why is it that those who are engineers or doctors or computer specialists that are more involved in such acts? Answer is not very difficult to find. Modern education as such is hardly based on humanitarian values and technical education, not at all. Thus they become technical experts, good engineers or doctors but have not much awareness about humanities. Their technical expertise is not tempered with higher spiritual values of love, compassion and wisdom.

These days education has become highly competitive and everyone wants to achieve at the cost of others. Competition, not cooperation, is the spirit of our education. And it is competition all the way – from degree to highly paid jobs. Widespread consumerism; and rat race it promotes, make people more and more greedy. They want more income, more comfortable life which comes only through often (immoral) competition. Humanity and human compassion is the looser.

Also, our modern education system promotes information, not knowledge. There is great difference between information and knowledge. Information is necessary part of knowledge but not sufficient for it. Higher knowledge always combines values with information along with deeper understanding of issues. As once Herbert Marcuse, an American philosopher in sixties who inspired revolutionary and humanitarian spirit among students and youth, said – our universities are centers of acknowledgement, no more centers of knowledge and they are centers of recognition, no more centers of cognition.

The university degrees thus no more provides in depth understanding and humanitarian perspective but only sufficient information for students to obtain a technical job. Such people can easily be swayed by campaigns of hatred especially if it also gives them sense of some 'higher cause.' Many supporters of Hindutva in USA are also highly qualified people who are made to think Hindus are suffering 'injustice' in their own country due to minority aggressiveness. And thus they finance Sangh Parivar in India.

Such an ideology of hate becomes more deadly, if the youth happen to come an authoritarian culture where there are no basic freedoms in the society. There are no avenues of protest available except to take to violence and much more so if violence can be justified ideologically as in the case of 'jihadi Islam'. Such anger is expressed through acts of violence (ideologically justified) in places where they feel great injustice is being done to members of their community.

It is important to note that terrorist attacks are taking place mainly in countries like USA and U.K. which were involved in committing aggression against Afghanistan and Iraq. Why countries of Western Europe like France, Germany, Italy etc. are not being targeted? Because these countries not only refused to join USA and U.K. in attacking Afghanistan and Iraq but had serious reservations of their own.

Australia's citizens also paid with their lives in terror attack in Bali a few years ago because Australia also jumped to extend its support to US war of aggression against Iraq and sent its troops. Now an Australian minister admitted that it was mistake on the part of Australia to have supported Iraq war because we thought we too will get share in Iraqi oil. Thus these terror attacks, however condemnable, have justification of their own in the eyes of these young terrorists.

The timing of terror attack in Central London and Glasgow airport is also important. Blair had just resigned and Gordon Brown had taken over. Perhaps it was warning to Mr. Gordon Brown that he should keep his hands off Iraq and withdraw British forces from there. Gordon Brown is not expected to follow Blair's policies and hence advanced warning to him.

Terror attacks can never be justified whatever the cause. Violence, however, important the cause, can never be justified. Violence is destructive of all values and totally brutalizes those who commit it. One cannot bring about justice by killing others or can never serve any cause. One must learn lesson from Iraq also. Shias and Sunnis are killing each other most brutally. It appears they have lost all sense of compassion for human life. While the Qur'an says that to kill one person is to kill entire humanity these so called followers of Qur'an are killing Muslims by hundreds.

Any version of religion which promotes intolerance and violence cannot qualify for being religion. Religion promotes nothing but truth, justice, love and compassion. Devoid of these values it could perhaps quality for political ideology but not for being religion. The Salafi Islam is highly intolerant and ideological and hence promotes narrow sectarian attitude. The Qur'anic statements about justification of war are highly contexualized and could not be read to use them for justification for killing innocent people.

Any innocent life taken by act of violence is a crime against humanity and an unpardonable sin against Allah. Taking revenge is not what Qur'an preaches nor Prophet (PBUH) ever urged his followers to do that. Qur'an repeatedly describes Allah as *Ghafoor al-Rahim* i.e. the pardoner and compassionate and Qur'an describes the Prophet as *rahmat li'l 'alamin* i.e. mercy of the worlds.

Then can such acts of terror resulting in loss of innocent lives be ever justified in the name of Islam? Those who brainwash these educated youth have their own political axe to grind. The USA killed more than a million people in Vietnam but did these Vietnami youth resorted to any such terror bombing taking innocent lives of ordinary American? Let those Muslim youth who become victims of hate campaigns ponder over this?

Salafi Islam condemns Sufi Islam but it is Sufi Islam which is highly tolerant, peaceful and respectful of human lives. The violence torn Islamic world needs much more Sufi Islam than highly ideological Salafi Islam. A great majority of Muslims in

India fortunately follow Sufi Islam and it is further tempered with by secular democracy of India and hence Al-Qaida by and large has not succeeded to penetrate Indian Islam.

It is doubtful whether Kafil has acted on behalf of Al-Qaida. Even British sources doubt this as the device used in Glasgow attack was rather crude whereas Al-Qaida uses much more sophisticated and effective devices. And even if it is Al-Qaida which is involved in this instance, it is an exception rather than the rule. Pakistani Muslims too love Sufi Islam but it is politicization and militarization of Islam which has made Pakistani society so violent as we witnessed in the case of Lal Masjid. Indian Islam, I am sure, will remain much more peaceful

15

Police and Minorities

The police as such is unfriendly, even antagonistic to people and much more so when it comes to minorities. The police act was drafted by Britishers in 1961 and its main purpose at the time was to suppress people and to enforce British rule. Thus the police act was meant to suppress people and make them obedient to the British rulers. It was understandable that any foreign rulers would do that.

However, what is most surprising is that even sixty years after independence from British rule our democratic rulers have not made any change in the police act. Not only that our rulers are not even prepared to implement recommendations of 5th police commission for some reforms and that too despite the Supreme Court directive to do so. The reason is obvious. Our rulers also want to use police for their political end. They do not want police to be people friendly. If police becomes people friendly politicians cannot use them for their personal end.

If police is anti-people in general, it is much more so anti-minorities, particularly anti-Muslim and anti-Christian. In riot after riot police behaves partially and does not hesitate to kill Muslims in firing. Latest example is of Hyderabad Mecca Masjid bomb explosion. The police fired ruthlessly on the protesting mob and killed six persons. It fired even on injured persons who were being taken to hospitals after bomb explosion. And what is worse they fired to kill and that is why six lives were lost.

Here I am reminded of terrible tragedy of Hashimpura of May 23, 1987. Hashimpura is near Meerut, which was rocked by communal violence in May 1987. The police as usual thought that Muslims are mainly responsible for communal disturbances in Meerut and decided to teach Muslims a lesson. The PAC (Police Armed Constabulary) went to Hashimpura and pulled out some 50 persons mostly young and some elderly. Most of them were poor.

They were loaded on trucks, taken outside city premises and shot dead and then their bodies were thrown into a nearby canal. Some two or three persons somehow survived, (the police had taken them to be dead), hid themselves in shrubs and escaped and told the whole story. It is twenty years since this terrible tragedy happened no action has been taken against the murderers. They are roaming free. Some activists worked hard to bring these policemen to justice but nothing happened. The state machinery was totally indifferent to this and not even summons were served to them.

Mulayam Singh Yadav who always claimed that he is sympathetic to Muslims and had an eye on their votes, did not do anything at all. Even today matter is pending and relatives of those killed are running from pillar to post for justice and the culprits roam freely. The reason is obvious: those killed were poor and also Muslims. Thus they were doubly disadvantaged. Recently on 23rd May on completion of twenty years of the massacre in Hashimpura, mothers, sisters and fathers of those killed demonstrated in Delhi holding photographs of their loved ones. One does not know whether the authorities took any notice of this grim tragedy or not.

The Gujarat police is of course notorious in this matter and they seem to get away with anything under the patronage of Narendra Modi. Sohrabuddin and his wife and another witness of the crime of fake encounter Koli were eliminated. All papers were faked under instructions of Chief Minister's Office of which *Tehelka* in its issue of 19th May, 2007 has given gory details. DIG police Vanjara called these fake encounters as 'Desh Bhakti'. Apart from Sohrabuddin and his wife Kausarbi, another Muslim youth Samir Khan was also eliminated in 2003. Ishrat Jahan and her colleague were also eliminated describing them as members of Lashkar-i-Tayyiba.

All these fake encounters were carried out saying they wanted to kill Narendra Modi. Thus Narendra Modi was trying to project himself as a martyr and a brave fighter against terrorism. He himself said in one of his speeches that he will lay down his life for the sake of the country and for fighting against terrorism. He said, challenging "the powers in Delhi" to "hang him till death" but has reiterated that he would continue his efforts and wipe out terrorism from Gujarat. "I challenge the UPA (government) to hang me till I die. If they plan to do this tomorrow, I request them to do it today, I will give up life. But I will not give up my fight against terrorism."

This is how Modi is trying to extricate from the fake encounter imbroglio. He wants to wipe out terrorism by getting innocent people killed. He wants to project himself as martyr by killing people from minority communities. All this is happening in a secular democracy. Of course Gujarat is a Hindutva laboratory and already has declared itself as part of Hindu Rashtra. Modi is showing all his efficiency in bringing about reality of Hindu Rashtra in Gujarat.

This clearly shows how politicians misuse police for their own personal ends. It is thanks to the Supreme court that Vanjara and other police officers are being brought to justice. Sohrabuddin's brother filed a petition in the Supreme Court and on being issued notice to the Gujarat Government, it admitted that Sohrabuddin and his wife were killed in fake encounters. However, Modi Government washed its hands off the whole affair and put entire blame on DIG CID Vanjara and others.

It is also true that there are some honest police officers who try to do their duty. Ms. Gita Johari, IG CID stubbornly refused to bow down to political pressures. Supreme Court had issued instructions to make her answerable to the Court only. But political establishment put pressure on her to report to her immediate boss Shri Mathur but she refused. However, such officers are very few. Most others are politically pliable.

There should be zero tolerance for encounter deaths and any police officer who has killed anyone in so called encounter should be treated as murderer unless he proves in the court of law that he fired in defense and that there was casualty on the part of police also. All details about how many rounds were fired and bullets fired should also be accounted for. Recently the Government of Maharashtra has issued instructions that there would be a CID enquiry after every encounter death. It is a welcome step. But one has to see whether this is strictly implemented. Many such instructions are issued but never followed in practice.

No other country ever tolerates such killings by the police. Encounter deaths were unheard of even in India few decades before. First encounter deaths were reported during emergency (1975-77) when some Naxalites were killed by Andhra and Kerala police. Mr. Tarkunde, (retired judge of the Bombay High court) the noted rationalist and human rights activist held inquiry in encounter killing and exposed those police officers who killed people. There was much debate in the country at a time and such encounters had almost stopped.

But soon these encounters began and many mafia dons were killed. But such killings were also not so genuine. Some policemen who became 'encounter specialists' were killing at the instance of rival mafia dons and making money. These encounter specialists accumulated wealth much beyond their known sources of income. Despite all this they acquired political influence and had direct access to political bosses over their immediate bosses.

Thus encounter deaths should not be tolerated in a democratic set up. In democracy human rights play very important role and police should be sensitivised to human rights issues. However, our police is still being used for suppression of people's rights and specially those of minorities. In most of the communal riots police hardly brings those responsible for killings of minorities to book. They do not investigate cases properly and even forge records.

One has to go through various inquiry commission reports to realize this. The Madan Commission Inquiry Report into Bhivandi and Jalgaon riots of 1970 lambasted the police officers for forging records in order to implicate some members of minority communities. However, state took no action against such officers. Instead many of them were promoted. Similarly the Srikrishna Commission Report which inquired into Mumbai riots of 1992-93 passed strong remarks against communalization of Mumbai police and named more than 30 officers for their crimes of omissions and commissions but the congress Government of Maharashtra took no action against these guilty officers and even where it did it was mere symbolic. And one such officer was promoted to the highest coveted post of Mumbai commissioner of Police, a person who was named for killing nine Muslims in Modern Bakery near Zakaria Masjid. Of course he was promoted by the Shiv Sena-BJP Government which came to power in 1995.

Thus the police force is both criminalised and communalised and is trigger happy when it comes to poor and weaker sections in general and those belonging to minorities. This is indeed a matter of shame and the state should make all possible efforts to secularise the police and sensitise it to democratic values. The police should not be used as a repressive force as during colonial times but as people friendly institution in a democratic and secular country.

There is urgent need to implement police reform and change the outdated colonial police act. Earlier it is done better it is to uphold democratic secular values of our Constitution.

16

Is BJP Reassessing the Muslim Factor?

The recent defeat of BJP in U.P. elections has given it not only a great shock but also has made its leaders review its policies. The BJP in U.P. was deserted even by the Brahmins, its traditional vote bank. Generally up to mid-eighties the Brahmins were voting for the Congress. The Congress used to win elections by getting votes of Brahmins, Muslims and Dalits. However, when the Muslims deserted the Congress in late eighties on the question of laying foundation stone of Ramjanambhoomi Temple, the Congress lost power and so Brahmins also deserted the Congress as there was no chance of its coming to power.

The Brahmins switched their loyalty to the BJP as it was raising the issue of Ramjanambhoomi and had much better chances of coming to power. The Brahmins continued to vote for BJP as long as it had potential to capture power either by itself or through suitable alliances. However, during the 2007 assembly elections in U.P. Ms. Mayawati was the rising star for number of reasons, one was her alliance with both Brahmins and Muslims.

Ms. Mayawati was following the well-tested Congress formula of Brahmin-Muslim-Dalit alliance to win the elections. She had solid Dalit base and had also convinced the Brahmins to vote for her. Not only this she had wooed the Thakurs also and was sure to get votes of a section of Thakurs too. The Brahmins weighed all this and deserted the BJP who had any way never fulfilled its promise to build Ram Temple. The BJP was, however, hoping against hope that Brahmins might vote for it but drew blank.

The BJP also tried to woo Hindus by not only its Ramjanambhoomi rhetoric but also by circulating anti-Muslim CD. It could not of course get away with anti-Muslim C.D. as the Election Commission took notice of it and stopped it from using it. This was also a moral as well as a legal blow to the BJP. Having lost elections in its own den is serious set back to its senior leaders.

However, there is no easy way out for them. To revive itself in U.P. in the absence of any wave in its favour is an Herculean task. With 20 per cent Muslims of U.P. hostile to it and Brahmins also having deserted it is under pressure to change its virulent anti-Muslim course. But that is also not an easy task. The BJP senior leaders in Delhi, nevertheless are thinking on these lines. A Mushaira (poetic gathering) at the home of BJP leader Shahnawaz was organized and many BJP leaders participated in it. Many moderate BJP leaders also feel we have offered Muslim votes to Congress and other parties on a platter by alienating them. We should woo them even at this stage.

Of course this will not be easy both from Sangh Parivar's as well as Muslim viewpoint. Sangh organizations like VHP and Bajrang Dal who even otherwise are accusing BJP leaders of soft pedaling Hindutva agenda will vehemently oppose this change of course. Their very existence will be in danger. On the other hand, after years of anti-Muslim propaganda, it would not be easy to carry conviction with Muslims, let alone aspire for the sizeable Muslim vote. They want to, however, convince Muslims that it was Vajpayee who initiated the Indo-Pak friendship process and also took initiative for solving the Kashmir problem. How far it will convince Muslims is anybody's guess. The Congress could not win Muslims back in U.P. despite all efforts.

It is very interesting to note that Mayawati, encouraged by her success in U.P. in getting Brahmin votes, is trying to woo Brahmins in other states too. The Brahmins are also elated by the U.P. experiment in as much as it has opened new doors for increasing their political influence by supporting the BSP. Recently the All India Brahmin Federation (AIBF) has decided to support the BSP in all future elections in its convention in Tirupati. It also wants to embark on a special mission to improve Brahmin-Dalit harmony. The Shankaracharya of Kanchi Kamakoti Peeth Swami Jayendra Saraswati is also scheduled to attend the convention.

Kotashankar Sharma, a Brahmin leader even commented that most of the communal tensions between Hindus and Muslims were due to the ignorance of and inability of the common man to see through the intrigues of vested interests. The AIBF conference is seen as an important event for Brahmins to become politically active again.

Thus the coming together of Brahmins from entire country to support Dalit leadership is a matter for great worry for the BJP. If this patterns of Brahmin-Dalit-Muslim alliance emerges on all India basis BJP will loose ground in other places too. After U.P. the BJP lost election in Goa also.

Surendra Kulkarni, media advisor to the then Prime Minister Shri.Vajpayee has been writing a series of articles in *Indian Express* suggesting that the BJP should woo Muslims to the mutual benefit of both. Mr. Kulkarni is even trying to prove that RSS has never been anti-Muslim and has been quoting from writings of Shri M.S.Golwalkar. In his column in *Indian Express* on 10th June 2007 he quotes Golwalkar from his interview given to Dr.Saifuddin Jeelani, an Arabic Scholar (*Bunch of Thoughts*, p-639) Golwalkar said, "According to our religious belief and philosophy, a Muslim is as good as a Hindu, it is not the Hindu alone who will reach the ultimate Godhead. Everyone has right to his path according to his own persuasion."

Kulkarni further informs us that specifically refuting the charge that the Sangh's concept of Indianisation meant Hinduisation of Muslims, Golwalkar observed, "Follow your own religion. The God of Islam, Christianity and Hinduism is the same and we are all His devotees. Give the people true knowledge of Islam. Give people true knowledge of Hinduism. Educate them to know that all religions teach men to be selfless, holy and pious..."

Kulkarni also quotes from Golwalkar to prove that Golwalkar did not support Uniform Civil Code; and was in favour of allowing Muslims to follow their Shari'ah law. He (Golwalkar) also maintained that "it is better that Muslims themselves reform their outdated laws and customs. I will be pleased if they come to the conclusion that polygamy is not good for them. But I would not like to impose my views on them."

Significantly Mr.Kulkarni says, in the same interview, Golwalkar warns: "Uniformity is a pointer to the downfall of nations. I am in favour of preservation of diverse ways of life. At the same time, we should pay attention to ensure that these diversities nurture unity of the nation."

Mr. Kulkarni therefore, is attempting to explore ways in which a fruitful BJP-Muslim and RSS-Muslim dialogue might start. One wishes Mr.Kulkarni all success. But he himself has been in journalism and a political analyst. Politics is not all about piety and noble sentiments, even if what Golwalkar said is true. Otherwise the RSS and BJP would not have been doing in their political propaganda that they have been doing.

I would like to ask Mr. Kulkarni that if M.S.Golwalkar was against Uniform Civil Code in early seventies why the BJP adopted it as its Hindutva agenda and still today it is on their agenda? Did Mr. Advani not preach Hindutva agenda at his aggressive best throughout late eighties and nineties? Were RSS leaders not aware of this? Or was Hindutva agenda formulated without RSS consent?

How about the textbooks taught in RSS run schools? Do they not spit venom against Muslims and grossly distort medieval history? If Golwalkar wanted people to be good Muslim and good Hindu, why Babri masjid was demolished and event celebrated? Was it being a good Hindu? Did RSS approve of it or not? Does RSS insist on Hindutva agenda or not? It often chides the BJP for not doing enough for fulfilling the Hindutva agenda.

How can one then have constructive dialogue between RSS and Muslims or BJP and Muslims. Did RSS leadership say a word in condemnation of what happened in Gujarat in 2002? A word opposing the Gujarat carnage from RSS leadership would have won over the hearts of millions of Muslims. On the contrary Narendra Modi became an apple of RSS eye. He has always been considered as an RSS man.

This is not to suggest that there should be no dialogue between Muslims and BJP or with RSS for that matter. But if Shri Kulkarni is suggesting dialogue at the BJP leadership's instance in the changed circumstances, let him suggest where and how to begin He must know that there is deep distrust between Muslims and Sangh Parivar and in the best of conditions it will take great deal of efforts to create even a semblance of trust. In any case even if there is possibility of any dialogue it is for the Sangh Parivar to take initiative and convince Muslims for a need for a dialogue. Writing such articles might be an exploratory process but much more substantial would have to be done.

A good beginning could be an apology for demolition of Babri Masjid and then an appeal to Muslims to come forward for a reasonable solution of the problem without hurting religious sentiments on either side. Such an eventuality seems nothing more than a distant dream for the present.

17

Conversion – a Review Article

Conversion is a highly sensitive act in today's communally charged atmosphere. Conversion is being declared a sort of offense now in many states if one converts to any other than Indic religions like Hinduism, Buddhism or Jainism. In a free and democratic India theoretically one should be free to convert to any religion, Indic or otherwise as religious belief is a matter of conscience and Indian Constitution guarantees freedom of conscience and also freedom of religion.

According to Article 25 of the Constitution everyone who lives in India is free to profess, practice and propagate any religion or no religion. Thus it is a citizen's right to convert to any religion of his choice, Indic or not Indic. Unfortunately the communal forces in this country (an even Congress in certain cases under fear of public opinion) are destroying his constitutional spirit by enacting laws banning conversion to non-Indic religions without district magistrate's permission.

It is alleged that the Christian missionaries are converting poor dalits and tribals by fraud and inducement and that large number of them are converting increasing Christian population and reducing Hindu population. This myth is being systematically spread as earlier another myth of conversion to Islam in medieval ages being spread at the point of sword, was spread.

It has now become highly emotional issue and it is so difficult to debate it objectively and dispassionately. But Fr. Rudolf Heredia has achieved precisely this in his book on conversion *Changing Gods – Rethinking Conversion in India* (published by (Penguin Books, India). Fr. Heredia discusses various aspects of conversion in a scholarly way. In the first chapter "Many Voices", he points out "...conversion can destabilize the life of a people, unsettle painfully balanced boundaries, scramble carefully constructed identities." He further points out, "If the affected people have imagined an exclusive nationhood for themselves, then nationalists will readily see conversions as subversive."

Majority communities are, particularly in democracy, are very sensitive to increasing or decreasing numbers. And this is much more so, if numbers cross certain Lakshman Rekha. And even more so if relations between communities is hostile. Thus Heredia points out, "In situations of sharp and hostile religious boundaries between communities, conversion represents the ultimate betrayal. Yet, even when inter-group or inter-community relationships are not in conflict, conversion movements have the potential to challenge accepted wisdom and renegotiate the status quo. No wonder, proselytizing is illegal in some countries such as Israel, Nepal, and most Muslim countries."

One can argue these countries listed here which ban conversion are or have not been so far democratic countries. Israel, though it has internal democracy, so far Jews are concerned, is, after all, a Zionist state and any way conversions are not permitted among Jews. It is considered as ethnic religion. Islamic jurists, though not Qur'an, do not allow conversion from

Islam to any other religion but allow conversion to Islam in the name of Da'wah (divine mission). But in India a Muslim can also, like others, convert to any other religion. Conversion from Islam to other religion is highly debatable issue among jurists. Many jurists argue, religion being matter of conscience, one cannot be forced to remain Muslim by coercion.

Conversion, it must be borne in mind, is not mere change of religion in most of the cases. It is very complex process and often involves much more than mere change of religion. It is also social, political and cultural as well as personal matter. Also conversion could be based on personal conviction or on some interests or may be a result of following a leader. There are very few who convert by change of conviction. It requires deeper comparative study of religion, one is converting from and of religion, one is converting to. Such cases are very rare.

Many conversions, and often so, are result of factors other than personal conviction. Some can change their religion in protest to or because of some adverse situation. For example, conversion to Islam in Meenakshipuram in 1981 was result of a dalit boy being insulted and humiliated by upper caste Thewars. About 100 dalit families converted to Islam in sheer protest to this humiliation.

In the increased political awareness many dalits put forward certain political demands and threaten to convert to Buddhism, if those demands are not met. Thus conversion can also be a political act rather than an act based on personal conviction. The right wing forces represented by the Sangh Parivar raised a political storm when conversions took place in Meenakshipuran and it was alleged that petro-dollar are coming to convert for which no proof, of course, was furnished.

Similarly all conversions to Christianity are alleged to be by fraud or inducement. Even those Christian missionaries who provide certain services to the downtrodden dalits and tribals are accused of doing so to convert them. Even an Australian priest Graham Stanes who was working with lepers in Orissa was burnt alive along with his two sons suspecting him of converting tribals. And on the eve of Christmas in December last communal violence broke out in the Phulpur district of Orissa in which several Christians suffered very badly and some were killed.

The Sangh Parivar, instead of being genuinely concerned about these conversions and engaging with itself meaningfully it tries to politicize the issue and tries to derive political benefit. All BJP ruled states and some Congress ruled ones too have passed laws banning conversion to Christianity and Islam (non-Indic religions) except with prior permission of district magistrate. One will have to prove that no fraud or inducement is involved in conversion.

Rudolf Heredia, however, instead of dealing with such controversial issues deals with the subject on entirely scholarly plane and deals with deeper issues involved in conversion. In the chapter on "A Postponed Tryst" he points out, "The debate in the Constituent Assembly on religious conversion illustrates the difficulties in legislating in the sensitive area of freedom of conscience and religious liberty. The Constitution adopted a sound basic secular perspective, though in a statutory document all nuances could not be spelt out, nor all consequences adequately anticipated." He further says, "Secularism is still an evolving concept and a much contested subject. Many consider it the single most crucial issue in our identity politics today."

Fr. Heredia is sensitive enough to the question of identity politics today and conversion has to be placed in that context, if we have to understand its controversial nature today. A pluralist democratic society (multi-religious, multi-cultural and multilingual) is riddled with several problems and its politics, be it in India or in any western country, becomes identity politics.

India's transition from monarchy to colonial society and from colonial to a democratic society involves very complex processes and secularism, as against what our founding fathers of Constitution thought, is too weak a bonding force in this transition. The way our society has been polarized today indicates importance of primordial identities. Conversions, in such politically charged atmosphere becomes hypersensitive issue.

As far as our Constitutional rights are concerned any conversion to this or that religion should not matter at all. Indian polity is basically secular democratic polity and fundamental rights of an individual do not depend on his/her religion and so if one converts from one religion to another, it should not matter. However, in practice, it is not that easy in an identity-dominated politics.

So Heredia points out, "The dilemma between individual and community becomes evident when individual and collective rights are not in consonance. Treating all equally could lead to some becoming more equal than others in violation of the rights of more vulnerable individuals. This happens in modernizing societies when the relationships between individuals are unequal, as in caste communities, where lower caste individuals are more deprived."

And usually collective conversions (or even individual ones) take place from lower castes to non-Indic religion like Christianity or Islam (more often to Islam). Today all controversies are related to conversion of low caste persons or those of tribals. In case of Orissa mainly tribals are involved. These tribals are under attack in many other states like Gujarat, M.P. etc.

The book also discusses personal journeys, those of Ambedkar, Pandita Ramabai etc. in early twentieth century. The chapter on "Personal Journeys" is very scholarly as well as interesting. Pandita Ramabai's case is of special interest as her conversion, besides being based on conviction (she was great scholar of Hinduism and also studied Christianity), had no political dimension. Her case also shows how complex is the process of conversion and social structure plays no less role besides conviction. Ambedkar's conversion to Buddhism besides being based on personal conviction, had also political dimension. Also, he not only converted himself but more than half a million Dalits also converted with him.

Ambedkar converted to Buddhism though he did consider Islam and Christianity as possible options. Had he converted to any of these religions, his conversion would hardly have been as peaceful as it was in case of Buddhism. Thus conversion is not mere religious but also political, as Heredia points out in the beginning of very first chapter.

The book is of great interest for scholarly and well-informed debate on the question of conversion to understand its various implications in today's political context.

18

Five Years of Gujarat Carnage – an Overview

Five years have past since the Gujarat carnage of February 28 2002 which lasted over six months. The carnage followed the burning of S-6 at Godhra on 27th February. It is great mystery as to who set fire to S-6 or was it an accidental fire? Before even news spread all over India of this ghastly incident at Godhra in which 59 persons were burnt, Ahmedabad city started burning on the morning of 28th February. In the post-Godhra carnage in central and north Gujarat more than 2000 persons, mostly of minority origin, were killed most brutally. Several women were raped and weapons inserted in their private parts.

The then NDA Government at the Centre and Modi in Gujarat maintained that S-6 was set afire as a result of conspiracy hatched by the ISI of Pakistan with the help of some Muslims in Godhra. The Modi Government arrested about 100 persons under POTA which was then in force. However, during last five years the Modi Government has not been able to produce an iota of proof against the accused in the 'Godhra conspiracy case.'

The POTA review committee opined last year that there are no substantial grounds for keeping the accused under the POTA but even then the Modi Government refused to release these accused.

It is real mystery as to who set fire to the coach S-6 or was it an accidental fire. The Banerjee Commission set up by Shri Lalu Prasad, the Railway Minister in the UPA Government concluded that the fire was result of short circuit inside S-6 and there is no evidence for setting fire from outside. Mr. Mukul Sinha, the defense lawyer thinks that fire was result of bursting of cooking stove carried by karsevaks had gone on long tour to Ayodhya. The Shah-Nanvati Commission, which is also probing in the train burning at Godhra has still not published its report. One wonders what conclusion it would draw.

Before even the cause of fire was known Modi pronounced the theory of 'equal and opposite reaction' and justified the carnage in Gujarat on the very first day the carnage began. Modi also insisted on carrying the dead bodies of Godhra train tragedy in procession in Ahmedabad thus providing direct provocation for the carnage. No administration, let alone a chief minister, would permit dead bodies of those killed in any sensitive communal incident to be taken out in procession as it acts as direct provocation for more violence. But Modi wanted precisely that.

The Gujarat carnage of 2002 was very different from other riots in post-independence India for following reasons:

(1) In no other riot in post-independence period chief minister directly provided justification for massacre as Modi himself did. There have been instances of chief minister not effectively quelling the riots but never of justifying them.

(2) In no other riot ministers and police officers led the marauding mob. In case of Gujarat carnage many eye witnesses named two ministers including Mr. Zadaphiya,

the then Minister of state for Home involved in directing the marauding mobs. He even entered the police control room and directed the police what to do. His cell numbers also have been recorded. No outsider is ever allowed in police control rooms.

(3) In no other riots police officers have been transferred for effectively controlling communal violence. In Gujarat 2002 several honest and committed police officers were transferred on this ground and soon after their transfer riots broke out in that region.

(4) In no other riots refugee camps were suddenly closed without providing either alternate accommodation or allowing the refugees to return to their homes and hearth. Modi Government closed the camps without any justification and without providing refugees any alternate accommodation or making arrangements to return to their homes and hearths. Modi while closing down the camps even derisively remarked that I cannot allow 'baby-producing factories' to go on, simply because few Muslim women who were pregnant at the time of riots gave birth to babies in refugee camps.

Not only that the refugee camps were closed down even today, i.e., five years after the carnage more than 5000 families are rotting in horrifying conditions in various refugee camps. Not only this Modi recently returned more than Rs.19 crore to Central Government saying funds are no more needed as all have been 'settled'. The victims of Gujarat carnage are unable to return to their original homes as they are still threatened by the VHP activists of the affected villages.

They say that victims would be allowed to return only if they agree to withdraw all cases against the perpetrators of carnage in the village and on condition that they will live in separate quarters like the apartheid and would not give *azan* on loud speakers. Naturally many victims have refused to agree to these humiliating conditions and are living in most despicable conditions.

What is most shocking is that the Gujarat society is still completely polarised and one sees no signs of repentance among those who indulged in most brutal violence against fellow human beings. They still feel the violence against Muslims was justified. The Sangh Parivar has been carrying on high-pitched hate campaign against minorities even today. Modi needs this campaign to go on as it be used a s political capital in coming assembly elections.

In fact the Gujarat carnage, as it is well known was carried out with the sole purpose of winning the 2002 assembly elections in Gujarat. When the Modi Government won the elections with two-third majority the BJP functionaries celebrated the victory by saying we have found a 'model' to win the elections and we will repeat it in other states. Even Mr.Vajpayee, the then Prime Minister of India when asked for his reaction as to the winning model, he replied 'will Muslims burn train in other place?' In other words even Vajpayee found the 'model' acceptable.

However, the BJP lost general elections of 2004 and Mr. Vajpayee accepted that NDA Government was defeated mainly because of Gujarat carnage. The people of India who are basically peace-loving and secular rejected the BJP-led NDA Government lest other states should experience such carnage. The BJP is in disarray ever since and has not been able to find yet its political bearings. The BJP and Shiv Sena are the two political parties which, thrive on anti-minority hate campaign. They want to base their victory in elections on hatred against minorities. The Sena Chief Bal Thackaray again made sharp attack on Muslims during the Mumbai Municipal Corporation elections.

Is there any way out? In Gujarat one does not find any way out as of now. What Gujarat needs in healing touch and only civil society can provide it. But as pointed out above, the civil society itself is deeply polarised on communal lines. In South Africa the blacks and coloured had suffered immensely under the White Government. When Nelson Mandela could establish government of people of African origin, he did not seek any revenge and instead set up a truth and justice commission. Bishop Desmond Tutu played very vital role in functioning of the commission. It provided the healing touch.

But one does not see any Desmond Tutu in Gujarat. The civil society is badly divided. In democracy civil a vibrant society can play very important role but when it is itself polarised on communal lines how can it intervene to set things right? Harsh Mandar, who himself is not from Gujarat, but is extremely sensitive soul, is trying his best to bring about some reconciliation is few villages of Gujarat. But it is only a lonely battle of an outsider.

Why the Gujarat society is so polarised today? The BJP has won over dalits, backwards and tribals in its political fold and thus Hindus, despite deep internal cleavages appear to be united. There has never been a strong dalit movement in Gujarat emphasising their own separate identity like in Maharashtra and other states. There has been no reform movement either. Thus in absence of such a movement dalits, backwards and tribals find it politically beneficial to be part of Hindutva parivar.

Only in 1985 the then chief minister of Gujarat Mr. Solanki had made a feeble attempt to unite weaker sections of Gujarat society by forming a KHAM alliance. KHAM stood for kshatriya, harijans, adivasis and Muslims. He gave them reservations as per Bakhshi Commission recommendations and won 1985 assembly elections with two-third majority. However, the BJP saw the red and launched an aggressive movement against KHAM alliance and succeeded in toppling Solanki Government. Solanki also unfortunately did not stand up firmly with the alliance and suspended reservations to save his government.

However, that knocked the ground off the KHAM alliance and except Muslims, other weaker sections sought refuge under the Sangh Parivar. That is the main reason why Sangh parivar has been able to successfully create the illusion of 'Hindu unity' and Hindu rashtra. The Congress after Solanki could not stand up and almost willingly conceded ground to the Sangh Parivar. Most of the Congressmen themselves subscribe to Hindutva ideology in Gujarat. It has rightly been described the B-party of BJP.

The BJP has been further helped by the identity crisis among the Gujarati NRIs living in U.K. and USA. They help the Hindutva movement in Gujarat generously through their financial contributions to compensate for their identity crisis. Most of the Gujaratis have struck it rich in USA and satisfy their conscience by supporting the Hindutva movement back home. Taking all this into account there is very little hope in Gujarat for the time being. Let us hope for better days in future.

19

Muslim Women in Indian Society

Today is 8th March, the women's day, a day which women celebrate as a day of their empowerment and a day of their rights. As I read in newspapers about achievements of women I painfully remember the plight of Muslim women in India, their lack of empowerment, their grinding poverty, their illiteracy and various restrictions imposed on them by their parents and husbands in every day life.

When I deliver lectures on rights of women in Islam, participants invariably ask me about actual plight of women in Muslim society today. I have to do lot of explaining the reasons of their sad plight. There are certain factors for which Muslims cannot be blamed like poverty. But there are certain factors for which Muslims have to own responsibility like imposing restrictions, which have nothing to do with Islam. These restrictions are rooted more in social customs and traditions of the past but legitimised in the name of Shari'ah.

Muslim women are suffering both from internal and external oppression. Muslim men practice what they themselves believe is Islamic and oppress their women and refuse to entertain any thought of change. Many educated Muslim women thus start believing there can be no liberation within Islam and seek their freedom through secular laws. I conduct workshops for rights of Muslim women and when they listen to what is written in Qur'an, they say they never thought Qur'an liberates them. They thought Islam enslaves them. Thus those who attend our workshops become activists for their Islamic rights.

Some problems Muslim women faces are of social nature and are common to women of all religions in India. All women face problem of social conservatism as they are reduced to secondary to men. Men are thought to be bread winner and decision maker across religions in India. But only difference is that among Hindus this situation is fast changing at least in urban areas. Women are becoming self-sufficient and, in some cases, also decision makers. But situation is not so bright as far as Muslim women are concerned.

Non-Muslims generally think Muslim women are oppressed and face many restrictions. This is largely true but matter is much more complex. There are reasons for Muslim women facing such odds in India. Mostly Muslims are artisans and self -employed and sociologically speaking they have restricted world -view and live in their own universe. Then there are those Muslims who live in rural areas and are engaged as agricultural labourers and related operations. They tend to be even more conservative.

These sections of society do not know what is written in Qur'an or hadith, much less what are problems with hadith or different schools of law. For them what imam of their masjid says is Allah's *hukm* (injunction) and must be followed else, they will be confined to *jahannam* (hell). The imam of the mosque also comes from poor family and has, in most cases, very limited knowledge of theology and Islamic Shari'ah. His 'fatwas' are based on ignorance. The 'fatwa' issued by the imam of village mosque in case of Imrana (that she should marry her father-in-law who raped her) had absolutely no basis in Shari'ah. The media also tends to give undue publicity to such matters.

Thus it is important to understand role of society as much as that of religion. Women are oppressed not so much by religion as by society. In order to bring about change in the plight of Muslim women it would be equally necessary to bring about change in socio-economic conditions of Muslims in India. If Muslims remain poor and illiterate, it will be very difficult to improve conditions of Muslim women.

Awareness for Change

It is also necessary to understand that things are not totally stagnant on Muslim women's front. An educated middle class is emerging among Indian Muslims – though still small – which is well aware of changing society and need for change among Muslim women. The educated Muslim women exposed to democratic politics, electronic and print media, are becoming aware of their rights and no longer prepared to accept what is being imposed on them in the name of religion.

In last one decade there have been many positive indications of change. A group of Muslim women developed a standard *nikah nama* (marriage contract) and forced the Muslim personal Board to adopt it. Though the Board did not adopt it as it is, it did respond to this demand and developed its own *nikahnama*. Is not very satisfactory to women but nevertheless the process of change has started.

It must be said that Board's entire functioning is reactive rather than proactive. I must say it is incapable of being proactive as it is busy defending medieval inheritance rather than re-think Islam like Muhammad Abduh, Fazlur Rehman, Ali Shariati and many others. They defend *riwayat* (tradition) rather than use *ijtihad* (assert intellectual capacity to reinterpret and re-think issues). Today when world is undergoing drastic changes, simply repeating, defending and stagnating will create discord between Qur'anic Islam and Shari'ah Islam on one hand, and Islamic Shari'ah and modern world, on the other.

Anyway Muslim Personal Law Board changes or not, women are not going to wait indefinitely. They are already on the move. Some Muslim women got together and formed their own board called Muslim women's personal law board. This board is asking its own stand favouring women on the basis of Qur'an and hadith. Though Islamic feminism has not emerged in India, it is on its way.

Some Muslim women NGOs have come together and formed Bhartiya Muslim Mahila Morcha. They have decided to operate within Islamic framework on one hand, and Indian Constitutional framework, on the other. It held its first convention in Delhi in early December. This is certainly a hopeful sign. Yet it is far from sufficient. It is just the beginning.

There is great need for Qur'anic literacy among Muslim women. Unfortunately the modern secular educated women know neither Arabic nor are aware of Qur'anic teachings. In order to bring real change in the Muslim women's condition, there is great need to have encounter with traditional Ulama on the basis of Qur'anic injunctions in respect of women. Needless to say the Qur'an accords equal rights to men and women and exhorts Muslim men of their obligations towards women. However, many of these Qur'anic rights were lost in the Shari'ah formulations in a conservative traditional feudal society. It is for Islamic feminist to revisit Qur'an and develop Qur'anic discourse of women's rights.

Most of the Muslim countries have abolished triple divorce also known as oral divorce. India is the only country with second largest population of Muslims, which still upholds validity of oral divorce and orthodox Ulama even uphold divorce given through SMS flying in the face of Qur'an. It is totally unjust to women and Qur'an whose most fundamental value is justice (*'adl* can never permit such unjust form of divorce. Qur'an has laid down proper procedure for divorce, which unfortunately is not followed by Muslims though they swear by divinity of the Qur'an.

India being a secular democratic country there is much more political and social space available to Muslim women in India compared to their sisters in many other Muslim countries. To avail of this social and political space increased awareness among women is needed. The greatest stumbling block is poverty. One finds even great urge for modern education among women but poverty pulls them down.

Mr. Firoz Ashraf, an activist from Mumbai for women's education, told me there is unbelievable poverty among Muslims in Mumbai. There is great urge for education, he tells me yet they have no resources and hence drop out rate remains high. He and his wife work hard to coach these very poor girl children to prepare them for SSC examination free of charge. Even then it is so difficult to sustain them on account of grinding poverty.

Another healthy change is that parents' resistance for girl's education is far less today compared to say 25 years ago. In many cases, Muslim women are far greater achievers in education field than Muslim boys. In Kolhapur, an industrial town in Maharasthra, I was told by Muslim leaders that there are twice as many Muslim girl post-graduates as Muslim boys.

Though one cannot expect drastic changes in the plight of Muslim women in India in near future but one can certainly hope for incremental changes. The number of Muslim women activists is on the increase as pointed out above. This will further increase with the passage of time. If Sachar Committee Report is implemented in right earnest, it will accelerate the pace of change in women's condition too But what is most unfortunate is that those who taunt Muslims about plight of Muslim women are today greatest opponent of implementation of Sachar Committee Report calling it 'blatant appeasement' of Muslims. One can very well see whether they are concerned with the plight of Muslim women or really trying to communalise Muslim women's issues.

To empower Muslim women, to reduce rate of child birth, to usher in religious and social reforms, there is great need to improve general economic condition which in turn will improve educational status of Muslim women and that in turn will bring in greater awareness for change. There is also great need for internal critique and at least educated Muslim men should attempt an honest criticism of condition of women in their community and consolidate efforts for change and reform. They also tend to be defensive and reactive. Time has certainly come to be proactive for improving Muslim women's status in India.

20

Islamic Shari'ah in the Western World

As the population of Muslims is increasing in western countries like U.K., USA, Canada etc. the demand for applying Shari'ah law to Muslims is being voiced. The Government of Canada was toying with the idea of enforcing Shari'ah law in the state of Toronto but none other than progressive Muslim women and men themselves opposed government's intention to apply Shari'ah law and in view of stiff opposition by these Muslims, government gave up the idea'

Now comes the news that the U.K. Government may also think of applying Shari'ah law to Muslims of U.K. the Archbishop of Canterbury has also favored this measure. Rowan Williams, the Archbishop is reported to have said that the adoption of some aspects of Shari'ah law in the UK seems unavoidable. May be Archbishop is extending hand of friendship towards the Muslim minority which is of considerable size by now and is seeking some kind of accommodation with Muslim leaders. Or, may be he is under pressure to approve of application of Muslim law.

The BJP in this country wants Muslim law to be abolished although Muslim majority in India is much greater in size than in the UK. At one time it was unthinkable for Muslims of UK to have Islamic law applied to them but fast increasing population is creating pressure on the government. Though as yet we have not heard any opposing voice from progressive Muslims of UK, it may be matter of time before it is heard.

If Islamic law as codified by Muslim jurists of medieval ages is applied, it will create more problems for Muslim women. Our 'Ulama voice stiff opposition to any change in the law in keeping with the Qur'anic spirit, it can certainly better the modern laws pertaining to marriage, divorce and property rights. But problem is our jurists and 'ulama are too rigid to agree for any re-thinking even in the sprit of Qur'an.

Also, as rightly pointed out by some commentators there is no single law. Islamic law is different for Muslims of different sects. Even Sunni Muslims are divided into various legal schools like Shafi'I, Hanafi, Maliki and Hanbali and in U.K. there are Muslims, following all these schools besides Shi'ah Ithna 'Asharis and Isma'ilis. Though marriage may not be much of a problem but divorce and inheritance laws can cause major problems in these different schools of law.

Though men will certainly gain but Muslim women will be great loosers, if one goes by traditional Shari'ah laws. The Qur'anic provisions were interpreted in medieval cultural ethos and women, in that cultural milieu was far from equal. In western countries discrimination on the basis of gender is a major issue and educated Muslim women mainly complain against discriminatory practices in the extant Shari'ah laws.

In all Muslim countries there is movement for change in existing Shari'ah laws and particularly women are demanding change and progressive men conscious of gender equality support them. If Shari'ah law is applied in countries like UK, will it be applied as it exists, say in Sunni schools or it will be reformed? If it is reformed who will bring about reforms? In India Muslim women are against oral divorce pronounced in one breath and 'Ulama oppose any such change. It is ultimately secular courts, which are rejecting triple divorce insisting on proof for divorce.

The Muslim women in India are also pressing for standard *nikahnama* which is perfectly Islamic as marriage is contract in Islam and yet 'Ulama are not agreeing to *nikah* contract favoring women in Iran too, there is women's movement and many women have been condemned to death by stoning on charges of adultery and the Islamic jurists are not prepared to effect any change in traditional Ithna Ashari law prevalent in Iran. Those women demanding reforms have been sent to jail. There is also *muta'* marriage in force in Iran which again favors men.

In Saudi Arabia there are much severer problems and women cannot even enter into business deal directly without a male member apart from being forbidden to drive vehicles. They cannot vote in elections also. Recently municipal elections were introduced in Saudi Arabia but women were not allowed to vote despite demand from women.

I have met many 'ulama in UK. They are as conservative as in Islamic countries, perhaps even more in the alien environment of UK and other Western countries. If any attempt is made to apply Islamic law in UK it will trigger off bitter controversy between Muslims and non-Muslims, on one hand, and between Muslims and Muslims, on the other. The Muslim women are bound to protest.

Large number of Muslims is from various Arab and African countries with extremely conservative background and if 'ulama oppose any change in Muslim law or its selective application and these conservative Muslims will fully back up these 'ulama.

Obviously, progressive Muslims wanting change in Shari'ah law will be outnumbered and the Government will have to listen to the conservatives.

Though there is provision for re-thinking in Islamic law called ijtihad, to this day 'ulama never allowed any one including one of their own tribe, to resort to ijtihad. An 'alim of standing of Muhammad 'Abduh in Egypt in late nineteenth century and early twentieth century had to face stiff opposition for his advocacy of change and re-thinking of Islamic laws. Though he rose to the high status of grand mufti of Egypt, yet he could not bring any change.

When the then President Sadat's wife Jehan Sadat used her influence to introduce a law by interpreting a verse of the Qur'an that a marriage would be registered only if husband bought a house in the name of his wife, it was removed immediately after the assassination of Sadat. Hosni Mubarak, the present president of Egypt also faced stiff opposition from the 'ulama of al-Azhar when he introduced a bill empowering women to obtain *khula'* (women's right to obtain divorce without husband's consent). He had to agree to a compromise formula before he could get the law passed.

This is the state of affairs in Islamic countries where reform should have been easier in totally Islamic milieu. How difficult it would be in non-Islamic countries, one can well imagine. In India where there are largest number of Muslims next only to Indonesia, ulama have opposed any change saying it is Muslim minority country and non-Muslim government has not right to interfere in Islamic laws.

When the Supreme Court of India granted maintenance to an aged woman beyond iddah period, the 'ulama, as well as Muslim political leaders, raised storm of protest and ultimately Government of India reversed the judgment of the highest court by enacting a law restricting maintenance within the iddah period. Thus UK Muslims will also face these dilemmas once Islamic law is introduced in UK or for that matter in any European and other western countries like USA or Canada.

The 'ulama consider formulations of medieval ages sacred and even divine. For them the Qur'anic concept of justice is secondary to men's authority over women. Men's right to divorce is considered as absolute whereas women's right is constrained by men's consent. Thus it is men who has authority to divorce although there is no such authority given by the Qur'an to men.

The 'ulama consider women as weak and emotional and incapable of taking proper decision and hence only men should take crucial decisions though women could be consulted. By the same reason they also think that a woman should not become head of state as it would be disaster for the state. This view is supposedly based on one hadith authenticity of which has been questioned.

Today there is great need for re-codification of Islamic laws and if Qur'anic spirit is followed in re-codification of Islamic laws in the areas of marriage, divorce and inheritance, these laws will be as good as modern laws based on the concept of gender equality and also much of the differences between various *madhahib* (schools of law) can be minimized.

These differences between various schools of law are precisely because of differences of opinion between jurists as also due to impact of local conditions, customs and traditions. Despite these differences all the jurists of the time were agreed on one thing: women are sinferior to men in every respect though there is no such assumption in Qur'an at all. This assumption of inferiority of female sex was introduced by the 'ulama and jurists who were themselves product of patriarchal ethos.

The Qur'anic injunctions on personal laws have no such direct or even indirect assumption and hence these injunctions prioritize women's rights. However, the right-based discourse for women could not be accepted by patriarchs of the time even though it was divine and hence Shari'ah laws were based more on patriarchal opinions and divinity was subjected to patriarchy.

Gender equality, originally found in Qur'an and lost in medieval patriarchal ethos has to be rediscovered buried in Qur'anic revelation and then only gender justice can be restored.

21

The Muslim 'Ulama and Status of Women'

The other day I read a news item in the Urdu daily from Mumbai *Inquilab* about the coming session of Muslim Personal Law Board. I was utterly shocked to read that Personal Law Board is worried that the Government of India has passed a law against domestic violence whereas our 'Ulama and *fuqaha'* (jurists) have always permitted beating of women. According to the law against domestic violence Muslim men have lost right to beat their wives.

Could there be any more shocking news about the status of mind of our 'Ulama, if this news item is true? Can it be right to beat ones wife? Does Qur'an or Holy Prophet's Sunna allow this? Did the holy Prophet ever beat his wives? Can anyone quote any instance of this? Is there any verse in the Qur'an permitting wife beating? Yes, generally the 'Ulama refer to one verse 4:34 which, according to them, permits wife beating. The translation of the verse is as under:

"Men are maintainers of women, with what Allah has made some of them to excel others and with what they spend out of their wealth. So the good women are obedient (to Allah), guarding the unseen as Allah has guarded. And (as to) those on whose part you fear ill-will admonish them, and leave them alone in the beds and -chastise them. So if they obey you, seek not a way against them."

This is the only verse in the Qur'an which 'Ulama hold against women. All other verses exhort men to fulfill their duties towards women and remind them of women's rights/ In fact entire discourse on women in Qur'an is right based and for men duty based. This above verse occurs in chapter 4, which is on women. There is no chapter on men in Qur'an. Qur'an emphasizes equality of men and women (2:228). About 2:228 Maulana Azad says in his *Tarjuman al-Qur'an* that this is revolutionary declaration of sexual equality 1300 years ago.

In the light of all this how can one think that Qur'an will allow women to be beaten? Now let us come to the word 'chastise them' which in Arabic is *wadribuhunna*. Now the word *daraba* in Arabic has several meanings. In Lane's dictionary one will find at least two full pages of meaning of this word *daraba* of which only one meaning is to chastise. Among other meanings is, according to Imam Raghib Asfahani, a distinguished scholar of Qur'anic terms, for he camel to go near she camel.

Thus if this meaning is taken then it would mean when she is persuaded go near her and not to chastise her. And this interpretation is much more congenial to the entire discourse on women in the Qur'an. Qur'an again and again exhorts men to be mindful of women's rights. Then how can it permit men to chastise them? And even when this meaning of chastisement is taken into consideration Tabari, highly respected exegete of the Qur'an refers to one hadith in which the Prophet only permitted very light strike with tooth brush or kerchief, and no more.

According to this hadith only symbolic light strike, so as not to injure, is allowed. But in the first place this meaning goes against the spirit of the Qur'an. All modern commentators have rejected this meaning. A Turkish scholar who has worked on the translation of the Qur'an for more than two decades maintains that *daraba* here means to strike out i.e. if a woman rebels against her husband then he should, in the last measure, remove her and divorce her as they cannot carry on together.

Another women scholar from Iran Laleh Bakhtiar who has translated the Qur'an from feminist point of view and has spent 40 years on this work also disagrees with translation of *daraba* as chastisement. She says, " After 40 years studying and translating books related to the Qur'an, I realized that something was missing: an objective universal and inclusive translation of the Qur'an from its classical Arabic into contemporary English. Most of the 17 English translations I had seen included some interpretation of the verse making a direct comparison between the English and Arabic extremely difficult. Plus, many of the English translations continue to use Arabic words and names such as Allah for God, which can be confusing or even off-putting to new readers."

Two things she says about the method she followed is quite striking: she has looked at all different uses of the word in the text in context before determining the appropriate meaning in English. She used computer to create database of 40,000 nouns and verbs of the Qur'an 50,000 particles of speech. This method is most appropriate as then alone one can understand the significance of a word, both as verb and noun. The methodology of understanding the Qur'an which I have discovered is also collating all the verses of the Qur'an on one subject and then inferring most appropriate meaning.

Also, one should always remember no 'alim (scholar) can avoid being influenced by his/her circumstances, both cultural and political, for understanding the scriptural text. There is no surprise, if the commentators of early Islam understood chastisement by the word *daraba* in their own cultural and political milieu.

Also, Prophet's Sunna plays an important role in evolving shari'ah laws. No one, even the most conservative 'alim or jurist, has ever referred to the holy Prophet ever chastising any of his wife even when they made unreasonable demands on him. The Qur'an itself refers to an incident in which the Prophet's wives made demand for more worldly goods which the Prophet could not afford. Let alone chastising them, he did not even utter harsh words against them.

He simply withdrew into a room and did not speak to his wives for a month and then, as per the Allah's instruction, explained to his wives that either they should opt for this worldly goods and separate from him or live with him and expect their reward from Allah. This incident has been referred to in the Qur'anic verses 33:28-29 and also in 66:1-3 and we find in Sahih Bukhari reference to this incident that Holy Prophet temporarily separated from his wives for a month and then reconciled to them.

This incident from Holy Prophet's life also clearly illustrates the real meaning of the verse 4:34 referred to above. That when wives rebel or try to become difficult, persuade them, then isolate them in bed and then reconcile with them and do not try to harass them or find way against them. Also the word *daraba* has been used in the Qur'an in number of ways and in different forms. For example in the verse 24:31 the word *daraba* has been used in gerund form for covering breasts with head coverings (*aurhani*). Here *daraba* does not mean beating or chastising.

Also, the occasion of revelation of the verse 4:34 as described by Tabari and Kasshaf, both highly respected commentators is that one woman approached Holy Prophet complaining that "my husband chastised me without any fault. What should I do?" The Holy Prophet thought for a moment and advised her to go and retaliate. This caused jubilation among women in Madina. But men were worried and rushed to the Prophet and said how will they control their families if their women retaliated against them? Then this verse was revealed saying men are maintainers of their families and if women rebel, persuade them, then isolate them in bed and then strike them away, if they are not persuaded, or according to Imam Raghib Asfahani, go near them after conciliation.

This verse often quoted by men for license to beat their wives but this meaning is not at all in keeping with the Qur'anic spirit. I would urge upon the 'Ulama to revisit this verse in the entire Qur'anic context and reinterpret it. After revelation of the verse 4:34 women came to the Prophet and inquired if they have inferior status to that of men. The Prophet (PBUH) replied I will wait for Allah's revelation. And then he received concerned revelation in verse 33:35, which reiterates that men and women are equal in every respect and that they will be equally rewarded for their spiritual merits.

Thus the verse 33:35 settles the matter conclusively. This is the last verse in respect of men and women. Also, while referring to relation between husband and wife (though the Qur'an does not use the word husband and wife, as the word husband denoted authority but only *zawj* and *zawja* i.e. one of the couple again denoting equality between the two) Qur'an says Allah has created love and compassion between them. It also says in the same verse that Allah has created your mate so that you find peace of mind in them.

If Allah has created love and compassion and source of peace in women how can it ever permit beating of wives? Thus one has to take all verses on the subject and read them together to find the real intention of the Qur'an. Chastisement was inferred by the medieval scholars under the influence of their patriarchal cultural milieu. One can discover new meanings as Qur'anic words are pregnant with many meanings, each meaning to be discovered in different circumstances but in keeping with the Qur'anic principles and values.

It will not only be unfortunate if Muslim Personal Law Board opposes domestic violence bill, it will also bring Islam to ridicule. And they will injure the real spirit of Qur'an and Sunnah. Islam greatly raised the status of women more than 1400 years ago and unfortunately our 'Ulama (though not all) still understand the Qur'an in ways which denigrates position of women as during pre-Islamic days which Qur'an describes as *jahiliyyah* (period of ignorance) and Qur'an came to dispel *jahilliyah* and create enlightenment. Will our 'Ulama choose ignorance over enlightenment?

22

U.P. Elections – a Proof of Mature Democracy

The election results from U.P. have stunned even great pundits. All predictions by observers and analysts as well as exit polls have gone wrong. Everyone thought that there will be fractured mandate and that BSP will go no further than 150 seats. Some said that Mayawati will once again align with the BJP in order to become Chief Minister. Some said that Mulayamsingh will align with BJP, in order to avoid being arrested by the Mayawati Government. The BJP was, on the other hand, projecting itself as one who will form next government and projected Kalyan Singh as its chief ministerial candidate.

The people proved all these tall predictions wrong and gave Mayawati their clear mandate to rule. They were fed up with opportunistic alliances and horse-trading. The way earlier governments were formed by MLAs selling themselves to the highest bidders had angered people. Even the Election Commission was expecting fractured mandate and had required all elected MLAs to be carted away to a safe place to avoid horse trading. However, that was not to be and Mayawati romped home with simple but clear majority.

The U.P. result is significant for reasons more than one. Mayawati really succeeded in social engineering, which is inclusive, and not exclusive. Her earlier political stance was quite exclusive, to exclude all save Dalits. She aimed at on Dalit votes which she almost monopolizes. Mualayamsingh Yadav followed MY (Muslims and Yadavs) formula excluding other castes and communities. BJP of course aims at completely excluding Muslims and not only excluding them but to target them for their hate propaganda.

In U.P., since Dalit votes were monopolized by the BSP, the Congress too wanted to win some seats by aiming votes of Muslims and a section of Brahmins. Thus all parties aimed at sections of society excluding others. This time Mayawati showed far greater maturity and pursued inclusivistic politics by giving tickets to Brahmins, Banias, Thakurs, Muslims and of course Dalits. This integrative approach won her rich dividends and she could sail through to chair of power.

The elections in India have deviated from democratic course and have become instead an exercise in creating divisive vote banks. Each party counts on support of one or combination of castes and communities and thus sanctifies identities and also creates clash among them. In pluralistic democracy like that of India, politics should be integrative and not divisive.

Credit must also go to election commission, which ensured absolutely fair elections and did not provide any opportunity for rigging or booth capturing. This was another landmark election after the J&K election. Such fairness increases people's faith in democratic processes. The election commission, one wishes, remains steadfast in conducting elections with such record fairness.

It is also praiseworthy on the part of election commission that as soon it received the complaint about CD prepared by

BJP which spewed poison against Muslims, it immediately issued notice to BJP as to why action should not be taken against it for spreading hatred against a community. The BJP had to eat an humble pie and withdraw the CD and its top leadership disowned it. Now the election commission has asked it to apologize for issuing such CD. It clearly shows that the BJP plays divisive card and is enemy of national integration. For BJP Muslims and Christians can never be part of national integration process.

What is more important, however, is that it could not fool common people. People of U.P. where once BJP was quite poplar party, lost all its glamour and could not carry people with it on the basis of hate politics against Muslims. It got no more than 50 seats. It could once fool people in the name of Ramjanambhoomi movement. It no longer works, nay does not work at all.

However, despite such humiliating rejection by people, the RSS maintained that BJP lost because it did not effectively pursue the Hindutva politics. The communal CD was height of Hindutva politics. It was clandestinely shown in peoples houses. It did its best to pursue Hindutva politics. Even the Yogi from Gorakhpur also withdrew his candidates from all the constituencies of eastern U.P. in favor of BJP and VHP, forgetting all its 'differences' with BJP appealed its followers to vote for BJP and yet it did not help. The credit really goes to the people of U.P.

Muslims too voted very wisely and though some Muslim leaders formed a separate United Democratic Front and decided to field its own candidates but realized that they may not draw votes and hence withdrew in favor of Samajwadi party. The Muslims voted for secular candidates, those who could defeat communal ones. This certainly helped BSP.

It is also very interesting to note that Haji Yaqub Qureshi was defeated. He tried to play the fundamentalist card and announced reward of Rs. 51 crore on the head of the cartoonist who had caricatured the Prophet of Islam. As the Hindus could not be fooled by the BJP's hate politics, the Muslims refused to be tricked into voting for Haji Ayub Qureshi. This is one more proof of maturity and understanding of the voters.

The BSP was quite fair in distributing tickets to various castes and communities. It gave ticket to 61 Muslims and got 30 of them elected. On the SP ticket 20 candidates won. Thus there are in all 56 Muslim MLAs out of 402 which is though little less than proportion of their population but is not a bad number after all. She has accommodated various castes and communities in her cabinet too.

There are in all 5 Muslims, 7 Brahmins and 7 Thakurs, 19 Dalits and 11 OBCs. No doubt she has given lion's share to Dalits but she needs to do that as it is mainly Dalit Party and she needs to cater to her main constituency. She managed to get 30.28 percent votes whereas SP got 25.45 percent and BJP was stuck with only 17.01 percent. Thus BJP getting such a low percentage in the cow belt is indeed matter of great worry for it. Though it is too early to say that now voters do not vote on the basis of caste and communal identity, but Mayawati experiment in rainbow coalition of castes and communities clearly shows that one can manage to get votes, if one clearly aims at reflecting the social diversity, of all castes and communities. This has to be promoted in order to cater to our social diversity.

Another lesson one has to draw from last election in Bihar and this election in U.P. that no party can take for granted political support of certain combination of castes and communities forever. For several decades the Congress had its support base among Brahmins, Muslims and Dalits but it came apart in eighties and Congress lost power. Then the Congress in Gujarat in 1985 elections under the leadership of Solanki tried combination of Kshtriya, Harijan and Muslims (KHAM) but it did not last beyond one election as Solanki suspended reservations for these sections of society immediately after winning election.

Lalu Prasad Yadav in Bihar and Mulayamsingh Yadav in U.P. won on MY (Muslims and Yadavs) formula. First Lalu lost in Bihar in last election and now Mulayamsingh lost in U.P. both had taken Muslim support for granted in the name of security but doing little for their economic uplift. Both the elections in Bihar and now in U.P. prove that security is important but not enough.

Neither Lalu Prasad did much for economic uplift of neither Muslims nor Mulayamsingh Yadav in U.P., except some promises. The Sachar Committee of course opened the eyes of Muslims and they feel no political party has really done much for their well-being. Lalu could win three elections in a row on Yadav and Muslim support but except preventing riots he disappointed Muslims. Mulayamsingh's case was worse.

Neither he could prevent breakout of communal violence nor he could ensure economic well-being and Muslims changed their loyalty and switched their votes to BSP leader Mayawati. Now people want results and cannot be satisfied with hollow promises. The U.P. elections have clearly proved this once again.

Two things are absolutely essential for contemporary India: reflection of social diversity in its politics and also assuring economic welfare for all through just distribution of economic resources. Also, it is highly necessary to prevent outbreak of communal violence. Any party which bases its politics on Hindutva or Islam should have no place in secular India. The election commission should derecognize BJP if it continues to base its politics on Hindutva. How can it be acceptable in secular India?

It is also necessary in as diverse a society as India that we do away with British system of first pass the pole method of conducting elections and make it compulsory for winning candidate to obtain 51 percent of the total votes polled. This will ensure inclusive politics and no party then will appeal only to this or that vote bank. The winning candidate will have to appeal to all castes and communities in his/her constituencies. The British society was almost mono-religious when it evolved this election system and we just copied it without much thought as to our own social reality. Sooner we do it better it is. Mayawati, one can say, has made some kind of beginning with her inclusive rainbow politics and this should make us reflect more deeply.

23

Policing and Minorities

Mahatma Gandhi had said that quality of democracy should be judged from the way minorities are treated. Democracies are participative system of governance but numbers assume great importance in it and when it is multi-religious or multi-cultural society, those in larger numbers tend to dictate to those who are fewer in numbers. It has been termed as majoritarianism. Any democracy which is based on the concept of majoritarianism, is qualitatively inferior. That is why Mahatma Gandhi maintained that real test of democracy is how it treats its (religious, linguistic or cultural) minorities.

But then everyone is not Mahatma, not even statesperson. An average person is motivated by his/her interests or prejudices. Most of the democracies in the world are infected by the virus of majoritarianism. Even western democracies treat immigrant populations from Asia and Africa in a manner which is far from desirable. They often remain on the margins of those societies.

India was multi-religious and multi-cultural from the day one in its history. Muslims were an important minority, even a ruling minority for few centuries but let us remember those who ruled were small minority within Muslim minority and had their own interests at heart, never of all Muslims. Overwhelming majority of these Muslims were converts from low caste Hindus, were poor and weak before conversion and remained poor and weak after conversion.

It is this poor and weak Muslim minority, which remained in India after partition to bear the brunt of not only their poverty and illiteracy but also of 'guilt' of partition. Those who were responsible for partition left the country to test its 'fruits' but Indian Muslims, remained behind to share its guilt and bear the brunt. Thus Indian Muslims have been suffering in different ways.

Majority communalists, and strangely even some rationalists, keep on blaming them for refusing to reform and become part of 'national mainstream'. This kind of civil society discourse, holds only Muslims responsible for their backwardness and illiteracy. They are supposed to be living embodiment of 'religious fundamentalism'.

The textbooks taught in municipal or state schools are no better examples of our composite culture and pluralist society. They are, on the other hand, worst examples of majoritarian ethos of our democracy. Thirdly, our media, especially, regional media, plays no less important role in disseminating raw prejudices against Muslims. Papers like *Samna* (Marathi), *Daily Jagran* (Hindi), *Sandesh* (Gujarati) and several others publish provocative material against Muslims and are read by millions of people including the police.

The lower levels of police officials, particularly constabulary, are deeply influenced by these papers, apart from textbooks and their family atmosphere. Some top police officials, are also infected and have to take orders from political bosses who freely use casteism and communalism as powerful instruments to fulfill their political ambitions. This was so obvious in Gujarat 2002.

Add to all this is the fact that our police is largely colonial in ethos. The British colonialists had created this police to suppress people, not to help them, to oppress and torture them, not to help them maintain law and order, to serve political masters, not to effectively check crimes in the society. But our colonial policing continues uninterrupted further embittered by anti-minorityism. Thus it becomes explosive mix.

From Mumbai blasts in 1992-93 to two Hyderabad blasts in July and August 2007 it is a long story of police inflicting torture on Muslim youth, mostly innocent; with no accountability. What is most shocking is that despite all this police has not succeeded recently in catching any real culprit. In Godhra train blasts too, all those arrested are not being tried in court of law as police has hardly any concrete evidence against those detained. Even experts have opined those arrested do not seem to be real culprits and charges against them may not stand in the court of law.

TADA was a monstrous law which was opposed by all human rights activists and which was misused to the maximum by all those who rule including the Congress governments but particularly the BJP rulers against minorities. After the train blasts in Mumbai in which more than 180 innocent lives were lost, the Mumbai police, has failed to lay its hands on real culprits, whosoever they are. Those arrested were inhumanly tortured and humiliated in most unimaginable manner before their family members.

Ms. Jyoti Punwani, a human rights activist and noted freelance journalist, exposed some of these cases. She was the lone voice of sanity. The national media by and large ignored these cases. Only the Urdu press focused on them. But Urdu press is read by Muslims alone. Now same thing is happening in Hyderabad after the Mecca masjid blasts and subsequent Priyadarshini Park blasts on August 25, 2007.

It is indeed a long and painful story of torture and humiliation of young Muslims from Hyderabad. A team of investigators constituted by social and human rights activists like Mrs. Nirmala Gopalakrishnan, K.Anuradha and Mohammad Afzal. They visited detainees in jail and also members of families of these detainees and prepared this report very painstakingly.

The whole text of this report is before me and it makes very painful reading. One is saddened to read this report and one wonders such flagrant violation of laws at the hands of their protectors, has been going on even sixty years after independence. Lower levels of judiciary and bureaucracy is no less insensitive to such blatant violations of law and victims and members of their families feel totally helpless.

Not only this, these victims and members of these families are so traumatized that they refuse to speak except in total confidentiality. Sometimes they do not speak even after all assurances of confidentiality are given to the victims and their families. The police even manipulates records of arrests or detentions. They arrest victims on slightest suspicion, torture them for days and then after several days will show them arrested or detained. The report under reference mentions several such cases. They were never produced before court within 24 hours as stipulated by law.

Most of them were detained illegally and tortured for days and even their family members were not informed. In certain cases habeas corpus petition had to be filed in the Andhra Pradesh Court as police would not inform their whereabouts. The Report, after meticulous investigation observes: "Many were picked up on flimsy grounds, kept in custody and released after many days of interrogation. For example, the Committee met Hafez Mohammad Bilal Muftahee, age 26 years, at the meeting with the families of the detainees, on 19-9-2007. He told the Committee that only reason for his detention (reason given to him by police) was that the police; wanted to question him about his association with Rizwan Ghazi. Hafez said that he had taught Rizwan a year ago. Hafez teaches Koran at the Royal Indian School, is from West Bengal and has been living in Hyderabad for past six years." The police came to his house on 2/9/2007 and had Rizwan Ghazi with them. Hafez was not allowed to inform his family. For five days he was interrogated at an unknown location where he was severely beaten, kicked, hit with sticks on the sole of is feet. After five days he was released. He was hospitalised and the records showed that the injuries he had were result of beatings.

This is one among several cases mentioned in the report on such illegal detentions and inhuman torture. Our police is generally very much against weaker sections of society, dalits, women from poor families and Muslims. When it comes to Muslims they are also motivated by their raw prejudices against Islam and Muslims.

I keep on conducting workshops for the police and experience these prejudices in the form of their questions. But I do not blame them as they are hopelessly ill informed and authorities make no attempts to train them in secular values and responsibilities in multi-religious society. Policing in multi-religious societies in modern competitive societies is highly challenging.

Media is also either prejudiced and justifies such torture for solving terrorist attacks (police has hardly ever succeeded despite such torture and indignities inflicted on people) or does not consider worthy of news. In the Hyderabad case also only

Urdu papers, particularly *Siyasat Daily,* a sober Urdu daily, was reporting these cases and the English and Telugu papers turned a blind eye to it.

Such state terror to counter terror by terrorist groups would never solve the problem, but would intensify it. The problem is political and has to be solved with justice and wisdom. All state governments have failed to solve Naxalite problem too, for the same reason. The police lets loose repression against innocent citizens and ultimately derive them in the fold of Naxalites. We will create more terrorists by letting loose terror against innocent citizens.

Are our authorities listening? Perhaps not, and will not.

24

BJP Enters Portal of Power in South

So at last BJP has realized its ambition of forming government in the South by installing its chief minister in Karnataka. And of course this became possible thanks to Deve Gowda and his Janata Dal (Secular). A political party which broke off from its parent party as the other section (Janata Dal United) had decided to join BJP as part of NDA at the Centre, itself ended up allowing BJP to stall its chief minister and fulfill its ambition of having its chief minister in the South.

There was time when communalism was considered purely north Indian phenomenon and south was supposed to be free of communalism. There were various theories about this. One theory was that Britishers who engendered communalism mainly through policy of divide and rule and taught distorted history in schools where it had direct rule like states in the north. In south, due to princely ruled states, British had no direct influence and such a distorted history could not be taught. Also in princely ruled states there was no direct competition for political power in the form of elections, society was not polarized.

Another important reason was Hindus and Muslims had same language and culture except in parts of Nizam ruled areas. In most of southern states like Kerala, Tamil Nadu, parts of what is now Karnataka and Andhra Pradesh, all spoke both in urban and rural areas same language and shared same cultural values. Thus it was difficult for communal seeds to sprout. In North besides other factors Hindi-Urdu controversy also played its role in communalizing the society.

In post-independence India too states like Kerala and Tamil Nadu were formed on the basis of language and hence Hindus and Muslims continued to speak Malayalam and Tamil Nadu respectively in both these states. In Karnataka, however, Muslims in urban areas spoke Deccani dialect of Urdu (in certain areas of Tamil Nadu too Muslims in some urban areas spoke Deccani Urdu but overwhelming Majority spoke Tamil) and there was often tension between Kannada speaking Hindus and Deccani Urdu speaking Muslims. When some Urdu programme was started on All India Radio there were riots in Bangalore. Bangalore experienced riots number of times. RSS also has its large office in Bangalore.

However, despite communal tensions here and there, Karnataka always elected Congress government. Hegde, a Brahmin, joined Janata Party and formed Janta Party Government but he was considered champion of Hindu-Muslim unity and Muslims in Karnataka always supported him. Unfortunately he also joined BJP aspiring for minister ship at the Centre but was soon marginalized and died a disillusioned person.

However, BJP was constantly trying to dig its heels in Karnataka and it found South Karnataka quite congenial for its politics as it is dominated by Brahmins. To widen its base it raised the idgah controversy in Hubli town. It insisted that Muslims should hoist national flag there though RSS and BJP never fly national flag from their own offices and always fly saffron flag. Not that Muslims were flying any religious flag there yet BJP insisted that Muslims hoist national flag. BJP leaders used to brag that they will make idgah in Hubli the Babri Masjid of south. Hubli also witnessed riots on this controversy and Hindu-Muslim polarization intensified. On every 15th August Hubli town witnessed communal tension and BJP encashed it politically.

Uma Bharti, the then chief Minister of M.P. came all the way from Bhopal to hoist national flag at Idgah and a case was filed against her for violating the section 144 enforced there by the District Magistrate. She had to resign on this issue from chief minister ship on assurance that it is temporary measure but she never regained it. BJP used this pretext to get rid of her. Needless to say BJP succeeded in widening its base by using this communal controversy.

Another controversy which BJP raised in Karnataka was Baba-Budangini controversy. Both Hindus and Muslims used to visit this place on the top of a mountain to pay their respects without any communal feeling. Muslims considered it as a seat of a Sufi saints who not only began to live in the area but also inspired his followers to start coffee plantation in this mountainous region.

However, Hindus considered it as a seat of what they called Dattatrey and paid their respects to him. But despite these Hindu and Muslim names there never was any controversy between Hindus and Muslims and both together visited the shrine and had great faith in the Baba.

But BJP saw a political windfall in this and used its front organization VHP to launch an agitation claiming it to be a Hindu shrine which has been usurped by Muslims. Again, like Hubli, they created communal tension in the area and increased their vote base. Thus like other places BJP constantly used such controversies to establish itself in Karnataka. BJP always thrive on communalism.

BJP is a single-issue party. It came to power at the Centre also by exploiting Ramjanambhoomi-Babri Masjid controversy to the hilt. It has no other issues and even if it raises other issues, it is just by way of compulsion in a democracy. Whenever it faces any crisis it raises some or the other communal controversy and tries to tide over that political crisis.

BJP reduced Gujarat to a Hindutva laboratory and polarized Gujarat between Hindus and Muslims as never before. It organized genocide of 2002 in Gujarat because it was facing very serious crisis and had been loosing election after election right from Panchayat level to Assembly bye-elections and re-established its grip through slaughtering, in most brutal ways, two thousand Muslims. Now Tehelka sting operation has exposed through the mouths of perpetrators of those crimes what heinous crimes they committed. It shows the depth of inhumanity BJP leaders fell in Gujarat to come to power.

What we hear from M.P. where BJP is ruling is same disheartening story. It is systematically spreading hatred against Muslims and communal riots are taking place in small places like Kukshi, Sanaver and so on towns which had not seen communal violence ever before. M.P. one journalist from Indore wrote to me, is in its way to Gujarat if nothing is done to stop it. These communal activities of BJP will increase as elections come nearer.

After what was exposed through tehelka operation in Gujarat such a party would have been disqualified from contesting elections in any other mature democracy. No democracy would tolerate such hate and murder politics to come to power. BJP does it with impunity and other secular parties, especially the Congress, keeps quiet for fear of loosing Hindu votes.

Now its communal politics in Karnataka over few decades has paid rich dividends and BJP has at last succeeded in forming government in the southern state. It celebrated this event in a big way. It mobilized teeming millions for the oath taking ceremony for its chief minister Yeddyurappa. Also, chief Ministers of all BJP ruled states including Narenadra Modi, leader of the Opposition in Lok Sabha, L.K.Advani, BJP president Rajnath Singh and other BJP bigwigs attended the ceremony.

Narendra Modi even suggested in his speech that Karnataka should adopt Gujarat model which of course sparked controversy. He was, people thought (and it may be true, who knows), he was suggesting, if need be go for organizing carnage like Gujarat to capture power by itself rather than depending on JD (Secular). BJP leaders, aware of what it could mean, immediately clarified that what Modi means is economic development.

BJP when it shared power with JD (secular) had played havoc and engineered communal violence in Mangalore region. The police, under the BJP MLA from the area, had openly played role in communal violence and police's role was also blatantly communal. The Minister of Education accused that Tipu Sultan undermined Kannada language and promoted Persian. Which of course was baseless accusation. But communal forces never care for truth. They thrive on false propaganda.

The BJP was doing all this to intensify communal divide in Karnataka when it was not in power and when it shared power as junior partner with J.D (Secular). Just imagine what it can do when now it has formed government and has succeeded in installing its own chief minister. One has to be vigilant.

The role of JD(S) of course has been most despicable. The former Chief Minister Kumaraswamy who was telling that BJP is communal and will communalize the state and that is why it is unwilling to transfer power to BJP not only agreed to install BJP Chief Minister but is eager to become Deputy Chief Minister in his cabinet. Indian politics is nothing if not downright opportunistic. It is such gross opportunism on the part of secular parties that communalism has thrived in India. It would have died its natural death after independence but for such opportunism.

Now secular activists should be quite vigilant and observe developments in Karnataka politics. Of course there are little chance for BJP-JD (S) combination to win elections in the next round. In any case JD (S) had won many seats with Muslim support and it is likely to loose those seats. And this prospects of likely defeat may induce BJP to go along familiar line.

25

Terrorists Strike Again at Hyderabad

Four months after bomb blasts in Mecca Masjid terrorists struck again in Hyderabad in the evening of 25th August at around 7.50 p.m. just when I started to go to Hyderabad airport after conducting workshops on peace and communal harmony and learnt about these blasts on reaching the airport around 8.20 p.m. It was a great shock for me too as I was elated that the youth, students, women and police had greeted these workshops with great enthusiasm. And it had such anti-climax that city witnessed such horrible carnage. I returned a very sad person though a few moments before I was elated at the success.

One could hardly expect carnage on such scale (41 persons dead and more than 50 injured) so soon after Mecca Masjid blast in the month of May 2007. According to the *Times of India* India has emerged with largest number of deaths in terrorist attacks. According to the *Times of India* figures in India 3,647 people have been killed in 3032 incidents compared to 1,121 deaths in 1,112 incidents of terrorist attacks.

However, it is not clear whether these deaths and incidents include those of North East and Kashmir or not. Probably it does. The question then is why India is at such a high risk of terrorist attacks? Answers given are on expected lines: India is a secular democracy and some forces from neighboring countries wish to destroy our secular democracy by provoking communal riots.

Second theory is that Indian economy is growing fast and Hyderabad, Bangalore, Mumbai etc. are emerging as growth engine for Indian economy and hence they are also emerging as centers of terrorist attack or perhaps combination of both these factors. Also usual suspects are Lashkar-i-Tayyiba, HUJI (Harkat-ul-Jihad-i-Islami), a Bangla Desh based organization or similar other terrorist organizations based in Pakistan or Kashmir.

Of course, these are mere guesswork. So far Indian police has not been able to catch any real culprits despite several major attacks like in October in Delhi, on Hanuman Chalisa Temple in Varanasi, July 11, 07 in Mumbai and so on. Still no one has been caught in Mecca Masjid attack also. Soon after such attacks the police points its finger at these terrorist organizations of Pakistan and Bangla Desh and starts investigations on those lines. Both in Malegaon mosque and Mecca Masjid blasts in Hyderabad, these organizations were suspected though to Muslims it appeared improbable, if not impossible, that Muslims will be involved in blasts taking places in mosques and in Malegaon, on the sacred day of Shab-e-Baraat, an important Muslim festival.

Just before Malegaon blasts and after it several explosions took place in Nanded at the home and godown of Hindu extremists and yet, police turned totally blind eye to these incidents and arrested, as usual, some Muslim youth, a doctor and others and extracted 'confessions' from them. Later they retract telling the courts that these confessions were extracted under duress from them and case remains unsolved. In all these major blasts hardly any case has bees solved.

Among political parties BJP takes the usual line that POTA or TADA must be re-enacted and only stringent laws will help curb terrorist attacks. Advani and other BJP leaders forget that during their 6 years rule despite these monstrous laws large number of terrorist attacks including one on Parliament took place. It is totally erroneous assumption that stringent laws will curb such incidents. Despite these laws, our years of experience suggest, terrorist incidents continue. Nagaland became comparatively peaceful only after political negotiations. Kashmir saw relative peace only after peace initiative was taken by Central Government and negotiations started both with Pakistan as well as with Hurriyat leaders.

Terrorism, let us remember, is a political phenomenon and can be effectively fought only through political initiative. The world has seen that how USA has miserably failed to solve the problem of terrorism despite its declaration of 'war against terrorism'. Both Iraq and Afghanistan are rocked with terrorist violence. In fact, tragically, it has become way of violence for the people in these two unfortunate countries. Pakistan too, witnesses horrible incidents of violence despite being frontline state in war against terror. Main problem is political, not legal and legal solution never helps.

To tackle terrorist problem one really needs, besides political efforts, to tighten effectiveness of intelligence agencies. Intelligence gathering is most essential part of preventive measure. In the case of communal riots also, more often than not, main failure of intelligence gathering. Intelligence gathering requires most competent and dedicated officers with commitment to secularism. Generally, non-competent officers are dumped there or these posts are used for punishment posting.

One will hardly find dedicated and competent officers. And even if competent, they are unwilling as most of them want 'better' posting with greater potential for 'earning'.

Also, the investigating officers should not have communal biases and should be ones with unambiguous secular commitment. If investigations are started on wrong lines on the basis of communal biases, as it often happens, there is very little chance of real culprits being caught. Innocent people are arrested on the basis of suspicion, tortured to give confession and then claim made to have 'solved' the case.

Thus the real culprits are never caught and innocent persons or mere carriers are caught. From my experience of conducting several police workshops I can say that police people, specially at lower and middle levels have very raw prejudices against minorities and at the top too, there are quite a few, though with more sophisticated, prejudices. There is hardly any serious training for secular orientation of these officers. Many of course come from direct RSS background. There is hardly any checking of ones ideological background at the recruitment level.

In both the Hyderabad explosions, the finger of suspicion was once again pointed towards Pakistan and Bangla Desh based terrorist organizations. In fact a section of the press has reported that bombs were made in Hyderabad itself. According to the *Asian Age* "All bombs were similar. About one kg. of slurry was stuffed into a curved wooden container covered with metal sheets. Iron balls bearings 2 weighing about 700 grams were found in the bomb". It is also pointed out that though slurry is commonly used by terrorists but use of curved container for powerful impact is not seen much, maintained an Intelligence Bureau official. A.P. Forensic Science Laboratory Director O.Narsimha Murthy said that explosive material in the bomb was ammonium nitrate (slurry) mixed with emulsifier. It was made by a Nagpur firm.

Thus there also could be a Naxalite angle as Naxals are active both in Andhra Pradesh as well as in Maharashtra in areas adjoining to Nagpur. All these angles must be kept in mind while investigating. Investigations must be carried out with an unbiased mind. Nothing should be ruled out in case of these terrorist attacks.

It is all the more difficult to tackle this deadly disease as ideologically inspired actors have no fear of death, much less of imprisonment. So many youth are unfortunately ready to kill and be killed without even a second thought. That is why in all the conflict areas around the world which have ideological dimensions many youth are ready to become human bombs.

In sixties and seventies of last century there was talk of urban guerrilla warfare by the extreme left ideologues. It had died down after seventies in the post-modern societies of the West. Red guerrillas had played havoc in many European countries like Germany and France as well as those of Latin America. But now left extremism died down but due to other political factors now religious extremists have become main players and they are wreaking havoc.

Now the terrorists are no more European or Latin American but mainly migrants from African and Asian countries and their European or American born children brought up in those countries. They remain alien to cultural values of European countries as they remain on the margins of those countries and never become part of their mainstream despite so much talk of multi-culturalism.

Of course causes of terrorism in Indian sub-continent are quite different but mainly due to political factors peculiar to subcontinent. Cessationist forces are active in Kashmir and North East on one hand, and those inspired by religious extremism from neighboring countries on the other. As far as neighboring countries are involved political stability in these countries is in our own interest. More the instability in these countries, particularly in Pakistan and Bangla Desh, greater the problems for us.

Thus leaders of our political parties will have to show greater political wisdom and sagacity, along with tightening of vigilance, to solve this deadly problem of terrorism. We will also have to win over confidence of minorities and let us remember anti-minorityism of communal parties and outfits is going to further aggravate the situation. It is in our own interest to keep our country free of communal hatred and respect religious as well as democratic rights of all sections of population.

These are some of the suggestions worth pondering and taking suitable steps to fight this menace of communalism. Complex analysis and complex solution is needed for complex problem. Earlier we realize this better for us.

26

Equal Opportunity Commission –Is It Desirable?

The Sacchar Committee Report also recommends setting up of an equal opportunity commission to redress many of grievances minority community has. The Report says, " The Committee recommends that an Equal opportunity Commission (EOC) should be constituted to look into the grievances of the deprived groups."

Explaining the need for such a commission the Report says, "It is wrong to assume that there is an inevitable conflict between the interests of majority and minority communities in the country. This is flawed reasoning and assumption." It further continues, "Deprivation, poverty and discrimination may exist among all SRCs socio-religious categories) although in different proportions. But the fact of belonging to a minority community has, it cannot be denied, an in-built sensitivity to discrimination. This sensitivity is natural and may exist among religious minorities in any country."

The Report, therefore, goes on to say, Recognizing this reality is not pandering to the minorities, nor sniping at the majority. This recognition is only an acceptance of reality...It is in that context that the Committee recommends that an Equal Opportunity Commission (EOC) should be constituted by the government to look into the grievances of the deprived groups."

The Sacchar Committee derives its model from U.K. which has Race Relations Act, 1976. "While providing a redressal mechanism for different types of discrimination, this will give a further re-assurance to the minorities that any unfair action against them will invite vigilance of law."

The Sacchar Committee Report, however, does not go into details of nature and structure of EOC. It has left it to be worked out by the government and its machinery. The Committee has also not thrown any light as to how will it differ from National Minorities Commission (NMC) in function as well as in structure. It is also not clear whether both i.e. EOC and NMC will exist together.

We can meanwhile make some suggestions in this respect. NMC, everyone knows, is hardly effective and has not succeeded in achieving its purpose. Its reports are not even tabled in Parliament and these reports are in no way binding to the Government of India. The people do not even come to know when the NMC submitted its report and what are its contents. Its reports are not even properly publicized.

Equal Opportunity Commission, on the other hand, as its name itself indicates can be very effective legal instrument to ensure that minorities should be ensured equal opportunities along with the majority in the country. In democracy all citizens, irrespective of their caste or creed or sex should have equal opportunities and our Constitution clearly provides for equal opportunities but it has never been observed in practice.

Despite constitutional provisions blatant discrimination has been practiced against minorities. And NMC is also toothless tiger and is unable to check these discriminatory practices in society. And in order for minorities to have sense of fair play and be sure of inclusiveness, EOC is badly needed indeed.

With greater literacy and awareness minorities are becoming more and more demanding and assertive of their rights. No democratically elected government can be insensitive to these demands. The universities are also starting new departments on exclusion and inclusion so that students can be sensitized to neglect of minorities and lower castes. This will further enhance awareness among minorities of being excluded from developmental processes.

India's fast growing economy is throwing up great deal of opportunities for jobs and entrepreneurship and if certain sections of population feels left out it can give rise to acute social tensions. These tensions can be smoothened out only if the aggrieved people have legal tool available to them to get their grievances redressed. It would have been much better if Sacchar Committee had spelled out as to what could be structure of the EOC. But we can say it would be an effective legal tool available to aggrieved minority person or persons for redressal of any grievance.

Besides U.K's Race Relations Act several other countries also have such legal instruments available like the USA. The US has Equal Employment Opportunity Commission. If it is proved that a minority person has been discriminated against in employment, he/she can complain and an investigation will be ordered and if discrimination is proved, he/she will be awarded due compensation.

It will be interesting to quote from Section 10 of EEOC. The African Americans, Hispaniacs and others are paid less than what white persons get for the same job. Median earnings for African Americans working at full time jobs were 75.9% of the medians for whites. The median earnings of Hispaniacs were 65.9% of the medians for whites and 86.8% of the median African Americans. There is also evidence that median earnings for individuals with disabilities are significantly lower than median earnings for individuals without disabilities.

Thus it can be seen that there is concrete measurement of discrimination in employment which the equal opportunity in employment commission is supposed to redress. Similarly if a particular community or caste is left out in employment opportunities legal redressal could be ensured through such commissions. It is a well-known fact that minorities are being discriminated against in employment of all categories from highest to the lowest.

It is also a known fact that Muslims and lower castes are not able to find accommodation in housing societies in big cities like Mumbai. Mumbai has been ghettoized and polarised in terms of 'castes and communities. Muslims find it nearly impossible to find accommodation in upper caste Hindu localities.

USA has a law to that effect too. The sec. 805. {42 U.S.C. 3605} Discrimination in Residential Real Estate-Related Transactions. (a) it shall be unlawful for any person or other entity whose business includes engaging in residential real estate-related transactions to discriminate against any person in making available such transaction, or in the terms or conditions, because of race, color, religion, sex, handicap, familial status, or national origin.

(b) It defines "residential real estate-related transaction which includes making or purchasing loans or providing other financial assistance for purchasing, improving, repairing, or maintaining a dwelling or secured by residential real estate.

India is far from such legislations. It is a well-known fact that Muslims and Dalits find it extremely difficult to secure bank loans or loans from any housing agencies. They are not considered as credit worthy at all and authorities demand collaterals as guarantee though they know the economically weaker sections cannot provide such collaterals. Though Sacchar Committee has recommended that Muslims be made available bank loans but even Reserve Bank and State Banks are resisting such demands.

Denmark too which has been recently in news for notorious cartoon controversy, has provisions for eradication of religion or race based discriminations. The Board for Ethnic Equality monitors Danish legislation, and the Documentation and Advisory Center on Racial Discrimination assists individual victims of racial and religious discrimination.

The Danish Parliament approved the first prohibition against hate speech in 1939, however, the wording was changed in 1971 in connection to the ratification of the UN Convention on the Elimination of All forms of Racial Discrimination (ICERD). Also, in 1971, the Act on Racial Discrimination was passed by Parliament, stating that a person commits a punishable offence if, while performing occupational or non-profit activities, he refuses to serve person the same conditions as others, due to that persons' race, color national or ethnic origin, or creed. The maximum penalty was specified as being a fine or simple detention or imprisonment for up to six months.

European countries are facing problems of racial or religious discrimination as people of Asia and Africa have been migrating to these countries in post-colonial era and they are legislating to ward off such discriminations. In India it is not the question of migration from other countries but minorities of Indian origin which have been living for centuries along with the majority community.

In a democracy such discriminatory practices cannot go on without creating serious political problems. The very fact that government of India had to appoint the Sacchar Committee to go into problems of Muslims proves this. But it should not remain mere elections gimmick but its recommendation should be concretely implemented to give substantial relief to minority community.

Of all the recommendations constitution of EOC seems to be most urgent with proper legal powers for the commission so that all discriminatory practices against Muslims get minimized.

Index

M